THE
PLANT-BASED
COLLEGE
COOKBOOK

Plant-Based, Easy-to-Make,
Good-for-You Food

Adams Media

New York   London   Toronto   Sydney   New Delhi

Aadamsmedia

Adams Media
An Imprint of Simon & Schuster, Inc.
57 Littlefield Street
Avon, Massachusetts 02322

First Adams Media trade paperback edition August 2020

ADAMS MEDIA and colophon are trademarks of Simon & Schuster.

For information about special discounts for bulk purchases, please contact Simon & Schuster Special Sales at 1-866-506-1949 or business@simonandschuster.com.

The Simon & Schuster Speakers Bureau can bring authors to your live event. For more information or to book an event contact the Simon & Schuster Speakers Bureau at 1-866-248-3049 or visit our website at www.simonspeakers.com.

Interior design by Julia Jacintho
Interior photographs by James Stefiuk

Manufactured in the United States of America

10 9 8 7 6 5 4 3 2 1

Library of Congress Cataloging-in-Publication Data
Names: Adams Media (Firm), publisher.
Title: The plant-based college cookbook.
Description: First Adams Media trade paperback edition. | Avon, Massachusetts: Adams Media, 2020. | Includes index.
Identifiers: LCCN 2020008676 | ISBN 9781507214145 (pb) | ISBN 9781507214152 (ebook)
Subjects: LCSH: Vegetarian cooking. | College students--Nutrition. | LCGFT: Cookbooks.
Classification: LCC TX837 .P58 2020 | DDC 641.5/636--dc23
LC record available at https://lccn.loc.gov/2020008676

ISBN 978-1-5072-1414-5
ISBN 978-1-5072-1415-2 (ebook)

Contains material adapted from the following titles published by Adams Media, an Imprint of Simon & Schuster, Inc.: *The Quick and Easy Vegetarian College Cookbook* by Adams Media, copyright © 2017, ISBN 978-1-5072-0419-1; *The Everything® Healthy College Cookbook* by Nicole Cormier, RD, copyright © 2010, ISBN 978-1-4405-0411-2; *The $5 a Meal College Vegetarian Cookbook* by Nicole Cormier, RD, LDN, copyright © 2013, ISBN 978-1-4405-5267-0; *The Everything® Pegan Diet Cookbook* by April Murray, RD, copyright © 2019, ISBN 978-1-5072-1117-5; *The Everything® Easy Vegetarian Cookbook* by Jay Weinstein, copyright © 2015, ISBN 978-1-4405-8719-1; *Plant-Protein Recipes That You'll Love* by Carina Wolff, copyright © 2017, ISBN 978-1-5072-0452-8.

CONTENTS

INTRODUCTION — 4

CHAPTER 1: PLANT-BASED COLLEGE LIFE — 5

CHAPTER 2: BREAKFAST — 14

CHAPTER 3: SNACKS — 48

CHAPTER 4: SANDWICHES AND SALADS — 78

CHAPTER 5: SOUPS — 112

CHAPTER 6: MAIN DISHES — 142

CHAPTER 7: DESSERTS AND DRINKS — 174

CHAPTER 8: STAPLE RECIPES — 204

RESOURCES — 229

US/METRIC CONVERSION CHART — 230

APPENDIX: GLOSSARY OF BASIC COOKING TERMS — 231

INDEX — 236

INTRODUCTION

Finish your homework.
Do the laundry.
Study for exams.
Cook a fresh, homemade dinner?

You might think cooking belongs at the bottom of your college to-do list, but it's actually an important part of college life. Healthy eating is essential in college, both to hold off any unwanted weight gain and to set yourself up for a successful, happy lifestyle. But how are you supposed to know exactly what to eat to look and feel your best?

In *The Plant-Based College Cookbook*, you'll learn how to focus on getting all the nutrition you need from all-natural plant sources, instead of relying on highly processed ingredients and animal products. The 175 delicious plant-based recipes that you'll find throughout the book can increase your productivity, improve your overall health, and even make it easier to resist those sugar-loaded snacks that temporarily raise your blood sugar levels but leave you feeling more tired than ever an hour later. And best of all, you can make them all in your dorm or apartment kitchen. No more microwave dinners or late-night trips to the vending machine for you! With dishes ranging from delicious pizzas to share with your roommates to classic chocolate chip cookies for a post-exam reward to party-ready treats like homemade tortilla chips and guacamole, these plant-based options can satisfy any sweet or savory craving.

You'll also find some advice on how to incorporate the plant-based diet into your busy college life. And just in case this is one of your first attempts at cooking for yourself, you'll find some helpful basics to get you started and make you sound like a pro—from essential tools and ingredients to key cooking terms. So get ready to embrace a new lifestyle that's easy to follow and provides the good plant-based health that your body wants, needs, and deserves.

CHAPTER 1

PLANT-BASED COLLEGE LIFE

Leaving home for college presents challenges as well as opportunities…one of which is figuring out the best foods to keep your body happy and healthy. An easy way to get the nutrients you need *and* feel great every day? Go plant-based!

In this chapter, you'll learn exactly what a plant-based diet is and why it's so great for your body. Even better, you'll find that it's also totally customizable and easy to incorporate into your everyday life, no matter your class schedule or weekend plans. With basic tips for adding plant-based foods into your daily life and easy advice to help you build up your kitchen, you'll find everything you need to start your plant-based journey today.

What Is the Plant-Based Diet, Anyway?

The plant-based diet is actually pretty simple: It emphasizes whole, real foods from plant sources. So, when you're looking at your food options, whether that's at the grocery store or in the dining hall, you really want to be choosing fresh, minimally processed foods.

What Are Processed Foods?

Processed foods are foods that have undergone a change from their original or natural state. An action as simple as slicing or roasting a vegetable turns it into a processed food. When foods are heavily processed, such as frozen dinners and packaged premade meals, they are often stripped of their natural nutrients. Even when vitamins and minerals that are lost during refining are added back in later—a process called "enriching"—the resulting product never provides the same health value as the foods when they are in their natural "whole" state.

It can get a little trickier when you start to think about what meat or other animal products you should include in your diet. Some people going plant-based will choose to completely remove all animal products from their diet, while others will only cut out meat. Others might just decide to limit their meat intake, while still consuming other animal products such as eggs and cheese. When it comes to the plant-based diet, a good rule of thumb is to at least limit how much meat you eat so it's no longer the main focus of your meal. Instead, think of meat as more of a side dish or even a condiment while you focus most of your attention on fruits, vegetables, and other healthy sources of protein.

In this book, you'll find a mix of recipes—some vegetarian, some vegan. So even though there won't be any meat, you'll have to keep an eye out for other animal products if you are vegan. The good news is that the plant-based diet is easy to personalize: You can modify the different recipes to suit your personal needs. Simply substitute your favorite vegan alternatives for any animal products used in the vegetarian dishes. Or try adding in some natural animal products (or even that small amount of meat) if that's what keeps you feeling your best. Just remember that swapping out individual ingredients will change the nutrition stats included with each recipe, so be mindful of the changes you make.

So, if you're cutting back on meat and maybe even some other animal products, what exactly *should* you be including in your meals? A lot of things! As you're preparing your food, think about how you're representing each of these major food categories:

- **Vegetables:** This should be a big focus of every plant-based meal! Things like lettuce, peppers, corn, carrots, potatoes, and more are great; you can use these ingredients to add a lot of variety and color to your plate.

- **Fruits:** Fruits like apples, bananas, grapes, and oranges are great on-the-go snacks and can be an important way to get the nutrients you need throughout the day.

- **Whole Grains:** On the plant-based diet, it's important to avoid refined and heavily processed foods…which means things like white bread and white rice are out. Instead, look for whole-grain options.

- **Proteins:** Meat can be a tricky subject on the plant-based diet, so you'll want to make sure you have other protein sources. Beans and nuts are a great addition, and sometimes other plant-based proteins are a good choice (look for options that are not heavily processed).

- **Healthy Oils/Fats:** Some fat is important in your diet…you just need to make sure you're choosing the healthiest options! Olive oil and avocados are great examples.

When figuring out how to transition to the plant-based diet, it's important to think about what works best for you and your body. You may also want to consult with a professional for more advice—check out the health services at your school or visit your regular physician if you feel you need more help.

Choose Your Food Thoughtfully

Understand that to get the most out of any diet, it's imperative to embrace the plan as a complete lifestyle change. This diet is not just about what you can and can't eat; it's about living for longevity by making more thoughtful food choices.

Why Go Plant-Based in College?

Changing up your usual diet might seem like a lot to take on with your already busy schedule, but college is actually the perfect time to start taking your health seriously… and the plant-based diet is a healthy, manageable way to do it. Statistics show that many students pack on at least several pounds during just their first year of college. And it's easy to fall victim to weight gain and bad eating habits through all four years of college as you work around a busy schedule, high-carb dining hall fare, and fast food at your fingertips. However, putting on weight will just increase the stress that you're already feeling from academic pressures, and it can be hard to take it off later. Luckily, the plant-based diet is a great solution!

The plant-based diet is a great tool for weight management and loss since it focuses on healthy whole foods instead of processed alternatives. It's also ideal for college students because it's so easy to customize to your personal needs and schedule. But more than that, it's been associated with reducing the risk of developing serious diseases like heart disease, diabetes, and even cancer. While some of those issues might not be on your radar just yet, it's important to set yourself up for success in the long term and keep your body healthy and strong.

You may even find some short-term health benefits—like increased energy, productivity, and ability to focus—due to all the nutrients you're adding to your diet. That can be pretty important when you're juggling a full course load, making time for extracurricular activities, and powering through some extended study sessions!

Tips and Tricks to Kick-Start Your Plant-Based Diet

The good news is that there are a lot of easy steps you can take to get to that happy, healthy sweet spot. If you're just starting out, you might pick one or two small changes to focus on over a few weeks. Once you get comfortable with those, try adding in some of the more challenging ones. Here are some ideas to get you started:

- **Plan your meals in advance.** Planning your meals ahead of time can save you from having to make yet another decision at the end of a busy day when you're already tired. You can even try meal prepping and cooking ahead. You'll find that it's much easier to stick to a healthy plant-based meal plan on a busy weeknight when all you need to do is heat up a dinner you've already made!

- **Be smart about grocery shopping.** The main focus of your grocery trip is going to be in the produce section…but don't feel bad about taking a detour to the frozen food aisle to help stock up on your vegetables. Using frozen food can be a great way to cut down on your cook time on a busy night and to find favorite vegetables during the off-season.

- **Consider locating a farmers' market or produce co-op.** Both celebrate the "farm to fork" mentality by offering locally grown foods. And, if you're worried about cost, you can often leave with a full bag of groceries for a fraction of what it would cost at your neighborhood supermarket.

- **Avoid eating prepackaged, premade foods whenever you can.** That doesn't mean you have to always skip the occasional pizza party or snacks with your roommates after a long week. Go for a balance! Do your best to choose whole foods that are complete as found in nature, since heavily processed foods are often stripped of their natural nutrients.

- **Stick to a regular meal schedule.** Your body needs energy throughout the day…and you don't want to wait until you're absolutely starving to feed it. Instead of waiting until you're so hungry that a quick microwave meal or fast food seems like the only option, a regular schedule can help you avoid those hunger pangs and encourage you to stick to your plant-based alternatives.

- **Think about your snacks.** Instead of stopping by the vending machine after class, try making and bringing your own healthy snacks, which can provide energy without the fat and calories in potato chips and chocolate bars.

- **Take advantage of the dining hall.** There will definitely be some days when you simply can't bring yourself to cook a single thing, so feel free to head over to the dining hall for a little help. Find out what plant-based foods your college offers and consider advocating for more if the selection looks a bit small. You can also check out what fruits and vegetables they have to offer (many colleges have a salad bar!), but you'll want to be careful of anything that's highly processed or may include undesirable ingredients like hidden added sugars.

- **Find a support system.** That might mean looking for support online or with roommates, friends, and family members. Reach out to others who have an understanding of the diet. By going on this plant-based adventure, you are looking at your food from a different perspective. You should be proud of your journey!

Figure Out What Works for You

As with any diet or lifestyle change, you don't need to be perfect. Start slow. If you find you're having a difficult time sticking with the plan, incorporate foods that help ease the stress. Find a comfort zone that works for you and your day-to-day life.

Start with the Right Tools

One of the first steps on your quest to go plant-based is to set up your kitchen! Start by taking inventory of what you have already and make a list of what you need. If you're in apartment-style housing, you might have a bit more flexibility, but in the dorms, you might need to collaborate with your roommates to cover the most basic appliances. Check out the communal kitchen in your residence hall—you might find some shared pots, pans, and other cooking essentials for residents so you won't need to bring your own. So, taking into account your own kitchen situation, review the following lists of basic items and mix and match according to your needs:

Bowls, Pots, and Pans

- A few mixing bowls for combining ingredients and serving noodle and salad dishes
- A few good pots and pans of various sizes
- A plastic or metal colander for draining washed, blanched, and boiled food
- One or two metal baking sheets for baking cookies or warming up rolls
- One or two glass baking dishes for use in the oven
- A muffin pan

Utensils and Tools

- One or two wooden spoons for stirring and mixing
- A heatproof rubber spatula for mixing ingredients and turning food during cooking
- A few good knives, including a serrated bread knife, a sharp chopping knife, and a small paring knife
- A plastic or wooden cutting board for cutting, chopping, and mincing food
- A vegetable peeler
- A can opener
- A grater for grating, shredding, and slicing cheese and other foods
- A pastry brush for basting food
- A wire whisk for whisking eggs and sauces
- A set of measuring spoons
- A set of measuring cups

Some college residences allow students to keep small electrical appliances in the dorm or the residence kitchen. A coffeemaker allows you to have a cup of java ready as soon as you wake up in the morning. Tea drinkers will want a kettle for boiling water. Along with a toaster or toaster oven, these items will help make your living quarters seem more like home. When it comes to larger appliances, definitely consider a microwave if your budget and college regulations permit it. Although it can't completely replace a standard electric oven, a microwave can be used for everything from making popcorn to preparing an entire meal. Compact microwave and refrigerator combinations, designed specifically for dormitories, are also available. Some even come with a small freezer attached.

Other Useful Tools

You might also find a hot pot, hot plate, or a rice cooker/steamer a huge help to cut down on cook time and counter space. Just check with your college's rules to make sure they're allowed in the dorms.

Many recipes call for food to be beaten, blended, whipped, processed, or crushed. If your budget is limited, hand tools can perform many of these functions; for example, a manual hand mixer is fine for beating eggs. And nothing beats a mortar and pestle for grinding and crushing nuts, herbs, spices, crackers, soft fruit, and almost any food that will fit into the mortar (that's the bowl-shaped part). However, if your budget permits, you may want to explore some higher-tech options. For example, a blender is perfect for busy but health-conscious students. Compact, inexpensive, and easy to clean, a blender will do everything from liquefy smoothie ingredients to purée vegetables.

Let's Get Cooking!

Along with those basic appliances and kitchen tools, you'll also need some staple ingredients to help you get started. A pantry stocked with basic ingredients—such as flour—will keep you from having to make repeat emergency trips to the local grocery store every time you cook a meal. Here are some essentials:

- **Flour:** Since white flour is heavily processed, look for whole-grain options instead.

- **Olive oil:** Olive oil is used for sautéing and frying, as a salad dressing, and in marinades. It's also a great alternative to less healthy options such as vegetable oil.

- **Vegetable broth:** This is used in vegetarian soups, casseroles, and other dishes. You'll find a variety of canned or boxed options in the supermarket, or you can make your own (see recipe in Chapter 8).

- **Dried herbs and spices:** Dried herbs and spices lend flavor to soups, stews, and other slow-cooked dishes.

- **Salt and pepper:** Standard table salt should meet all your cooking needs, but you may want to consider purchasing a pepper mill to grind your own peppercorns.

- **Miscellaneous flavoring agents:** Lemon juice, tomato sauce, and soy sauce will allow you to create a number of different dishes.

Store Your Ingredients Safely
Even dry ingredients go stale eventually. And, of course, improper storage will cause ingredients to go stale more quickly. Worse, certain types of small bugs—such as the flour beetle—feed on dry ingredients and can make your dorm pretty unpleasant. For best results, store your staples in tightly sealed canisters.

Once you have the basics, you're ready to get started! Say goodbye to daily peanut butter and jelly sandwiches, the same old pasta from the dining hall, and quick snacks from the vending machines. Instead, say hello to fresh, natural ingredients that will always make nutritious *and* delicious meals. Let's get cooking!

CHAPTER 2

BREAKFAST

Brown Rice and Spiced Peaches 16

High-Fiber Fruity Oatmeal 17

Sweet Potato Apple Latkes............... 18

Zucchini Bread 19

Pumpkin Muffins................................ 20

Banana and Chocolate Chip
Pancake Wrap.................................... 21

Banana Chocolate Chip Muffins 23

Cheese and Mushroom Frittata......... 24

Herb-Stuffed Tomatoes with Feta 26

Spinach and Ricotta Mini Quiches... 27

Vanilla Flax Granola........................... 28

Savory Scrambled Eggs..................... 29

Pear and Pumpkin
Breakfast Bread................................. 30

Toasted Nut "Cereal" 31

Very Veggie Omelet........................... 32

Sweet Potato Hash Browns
with Scrambled Eggs.......................... 34

Loaded White Bean Avocado Toast... 35

Savory Breakfast Quinoa Bowl........ 36

Vegetable Tofu Scramble 37

Savory Chickpea Oatmeal
with Garlic Yogurt Sauce.................... 38

Kale, Sweet Potato, and
Tempeh Breakfast Hash..................... 39

Tofu Breakfast Burrito 41

Vegan Pancakes................................. 42

Breakfast Tacos.................................. 43

Pumpkin Pie Chia Seed Pudding..... 44

Peanut Butter Cup Oatmeal.............. 45

Banana Honey Pancakes................... 46

Raspberry Breakfast Bars................. 47

BROWN RICE
AND SPICED PEACHES
SERVES 4

Rice for breakfast? Don't knock it till you've tried it! This is an excellent cold-weather breakfast. You can prepare the rice and peaches in advance, and heat them in the microwave. Add milk before heating if desired!

INGREDIENTS

1 1/2 cups uncooked brown rice

3 cups water

1 teaspoon salt

2 cups canned peaches in water
(no syrup) with 3/4 cup natural juices

1/2 teaspoon cinnamon

1/4 teaspoon ground nutmeg

1 tablespoon fresh lemon juice

2 teaspoons honey, divided

1. Cook rice in salted water until tender, following package directions.

2. In a separate medium saucepan, mix peaches, spices, lemon juice, and 1 teaspoon honey. Bring to a boil and set aside.

3. When ready to serve, mix peaches and rice, and drizzle with remaining honey.

PER SERVING
Calories: 324 – Fat: 2g – Sodium: 590mg – Fiber: 5g
Carbohydrates: 72g – Sugar: 15g – Protein: 6g

The Juice Solution
While it's always best to squeeze lemon or lime juice right out of the fruit, it's not always easy to keep fresh lemons and limes on hand. Luckily, you can buy bottles of lemon juice and lime juice that will stay good in the refrigerator for several weeks. These will come in handy in lots of recipes, from guacamole to fruit salad.

HIGH-FIBER FRUITY OATMEAL

SERVES 1

Don't want to feel weighed down during early classes? Nuts are a very high-fiber food with some good fat. Both the fiber and the fat take a while to digest without that heavy feeling.

INGREDIENTS

$\frac{1}{2}$ cup quick-cooking oats

Orange juice to cover oats
(about $\frac{3}{4}$ cup)

$\frac{1}{4}$ cup pecans

10 raisins

$\frac{1}{2}$ medium banana, peeled and sliced

2 tablespoons honey

1. Boil oats in orange juice.

2. When oats have absorbed orange juice, stir in pecans, raisins, banana, and honey.

PER SERVING

Calories: 604 — Fat: 19g — Sodium: 6mg — Fiber: 9g

Carbohydrates: 104g — Sugar: 62g — Protein: 10g

SWEET POTATO APPLE LATKES
MAKES 12 LATKES

A food processor helps with preparing the potatoes, apples, and onion for this recipe. But if you don't have one, a low-tech box grater will do the job. Serve topped with applesauce or nondairy sour cream.

INGREDIENTS

3 large sweet potatoes, peeled and grated

1 medium apple, peeled and grated

1 small yellow onion, peeled and grated

Egg replacement equal to 2 eggs

3 tablespoons all-purpose flour

1 teaspoon baking powder

$\frac{1}{2}$ teaspoon ground cinnamon

$\frac{1}{2}$ teaspoon ground nutmeg

$\frac{1}{2}$ teaspoon salt

3 tablespoons oil, for frying

1. Using a cloth or paper towel, gently squeeze out excess moisture from potatoes and apples, and combine with onions in a large bowl.

2. Combine remaining ingredients except for oil and mix well.

3. Heat oil in a large frying pan. Drop the potato mixture in the hot oil $\frac{1}{4}$ cup at a time, and use a spatula to flatten, forming a pancake. Cook for 3–4 minutes on each side, until lightly crisped.

PER SERVING (1 LATKE)
Calories: 93 – Fat: 4g – Sodium: 60mg – Fiber: 2g
Carbohydrates: 14g – Sugar: 5g – Protein: 2g

Egg Replacements
Several brands, such as Bob's Red Mill, make a vegan egg replacement powder. Simply mix water with the powder for an instant vegan substitute for eggs. Look for this product near the baking supplies in the supermarket, or order online. Other egg substitutes include flaxseed meal soaked in water. Check online for ideas and directions.

ZUCCHINI BREAD
SERVES 12

This hearty bread will give you the boost you need to get through your morning classes. Adding dried fruits and nuts gives a nice touch of sweetness and a pleasant crunch to this recipe.

INGREDIENTS

$1\frac{1}{2}$ cups all-purpose flour

I teaspoon baking powder

I teaspoon baking soda

$\frac{1}{2}$ teaspoon salt

2 teaspoons ground cinnamon

$\frac{1}{2}$ teaspoon ground nutmeg

I cup sugar

$\frac{1}{2}$ cup canola oil

Egg replacement equal to 2 eggs

I teaspoon vanilla extract

I cup grated zucchini

1. Preheat oven to 350°F. Grease a 9" × 5" loaf pan.

2. Whisk together flour, baking powder, baking soda, salt, cinnamon, and nutmeg in a large bowl. In a separate medium bowl, stir together sugar, oil, egg replacement, and vanilla. Add the wet ingredients to the flour mixture, stirring until just mixed. Fold in grated zucchini.

3. Pour batter into a greased loaf pan and bake 50–60 minutes until golden brown. A toothpick should come out clean when inserted into the center of the loaf. Cool in the pan.

PER SERVING

Calories: 210 – Fat: 9g – Sodium: 246mg – Fiber: 1g
Carbohydrates: 30g – Sugar: 17g – Protein: 2g

Vegetable Breads

This bread also stands up well to a variety of vegetable additions. Try grating in a mixture of carrots, yellow squash, and red bell peppers for a bread that looks like a slice of confetti. You can add up to an additional $1\frac{1}{2}$ cups of extra ingredients.

PUMPKIN MUFFINS
MAKES 20 MUFFINS

The perfect autumn treat to celebrate the harvest season and the beginning of the school year. If you've got the time, there's nothing like fresh roasted pumpkin! Make your own purée to substitute for canned.

INGREDIENTS

1½ cups all-purpose flour

1 cup whole-wheat flour

¾ cup sugar

1 tablespoon baking powder

½ teaspoon baking soda

½ teaspoon salt

1 teaspoon ground cinnamon

½ teaspoon ground nutmeg

¼ teaspoon ground ginger

¼ teaspoon ground allspice

1 (15-ounce) can pumpkin purée

¼ cup canola oil

¼ cup soy milk

Egg replacement equal to 1 egg

½ teaspoon minced lemon zest

½ cup raisins

1. Preheat oven to 375°F. Grease a muffin tin or line with paper muffin cups.

2. In a large bowl, combine flours, sugar, baking powder, baking soda, salt, cinnamon, nutmeg, ginger, and allspice. In a separate medium bowl, mix pumpkin purée, oil, soy milk, egg replacement, and lemon zest. Add to the flour mixture, stirring until just mixed. Fold in raisins.

3. Pour batter into prepared muffin tins up to two-thirds full.

4. Bake 25–35 minutes or until a toothpick inserted into the center of a muffin comes out clean. Remove from pan to cool.

PER MUFFIN
Calories: 131 – Fat: 3g – Sodium: 108mg – Fiber: 2g
Carbohydrates: 24g – Sugar: 11g – Protein: 2g

Ditch the Can

To make pumpkin purée, carefully chop your pumpkin in half, remove the seeds (save and toast those later!), and place cut-side down in a large baking dish. Pour about ¼" of water into the bottom of the dish and roast for 45–60 minutes in a 375°F oven. Cool, then peel off and discard the skin. Mash or purée the flesh until smooth. Whatever you don't use will keep in the freezer for next time.

BANANA AND CHOCOLATE CHIP PANCAKE WRAP

MAKES 4 PANCAKES

The chocolate chips sweeten this pancake recipe and are best when applied immediately after you take the pancakes off the griddle so they start to melt into the pancakes. Add walnuts to the recipe for an extra boost of protein.

INGREDIENTS

$\frac{1}{2}$ cup dry instant oatmeal

$\frac{1}{2}$ cup cottage cheese

3 medium egg whites

2 tablespoons sugar

1 teaspoon ground cinnamon

1 teaspoon vanilla extract

1 medium banana, peeled

$\frac{1}{4}$ cup semisweet chocolate chips

1. Combine oatmeal, cottage cheese, egg whites, sugar, cinnamon, and vanilla in a blender until smooth.

2. Mash banana in a bowl and fold into pancake mix.

3. Pour four individual pancakes on a large skillet, thinly.

4. Remove from the skillet and place a few chocolate chips on each pancake. Fold over like a wrap.

PER PANCAKE
Calories: 186 – Fat: 5g – Sodium: 145mg – Fiber: 3g
Carbohydrates: 29g – Sugar: 17g – Protein: 8g

BANANA CHOCOLATE CHIP MUFFINS

MAKES 18 MUFFINS

Make these muffins ahead of time to take to your morning classes. To freeze, wrap tightly in aluminum foil or place in a resealable plastic bag. To reheat, microwave briefly on high heat or warm in a 300°F oven for 15–20 minutes.

INGREDIENTS

$\frac{1}{2}$ cup soy milk

1 teaspoon lemon juice

$\frac{3}{4}$ cup brown sugar

$\frac{1}{2}$ cup vegan margarine, softened at room temperature

3 medium bananas, peeled and mashed

1 teaspoon vanilla extract

$2\frac{1}{4}$ cups all-purpose flour

1 cup whole-wheat flour

$\frac{1}{2}$ teaspoon baking powder

$\frac{1}{2}$ teaspoon baking soda

$\frac{1}{4}$ teaspoon salt

1 cup coarsely chopped vegan chocolate chips

$\frac{1}{2}$ cup chopped walnuts

1. Preheat oven to 350°F. Grease a muffin tin or line with paper muffin cups.

2. In a small bowl, stir soy milk and lemon juice together and allow to sit 10 minutes.

3. In a large bowl, cream brown sugar and margarine together until fluffy. Stir in banana, vanilla extract, and soy milk mixture until blended.

4. In a separate large bowl, whisk together flours, baking powder, baking soda, and salt. Add the flour mixture to the wet ingredients, stirring until just mixed. Fold in chocolate chips and walnuts.

5. Pour batter into prepared muffin tins up to two-thirds full.

6. Bake muffins 20–25 minutes or until a toothpick comes out clean when inserted into the center of a muffin. Cool in the pan 10 minutes, then transfer to wire racks. Cool completely.

PER SERVING (1 MUFFIN)

Calories: 248 – Fat: 9g – Sodium: 122mg – Fiber: 3g

Carbohydrates: 38g – Sugar: 17g – Protein: 4g

CHEESE AND MUSHROOM FRITTATA

SERVES 4

This is a perfect main-course dish for a brunch with your roomies! Make ahead and serve at room temperature. It's also a perfect way to utilize leftover vegetables of all sorts—add any you like!

INGREDIENTS

4 tablespoons olive oil, divided

6 large button mushrooms, sliced (about $1\frac{1}{4}$ cups)

$\frac{1}{2}$ cup chopped white onion

3 large eggs

$\frac{1}{2}$ cup whole milk

$\frac{1}{8}$ teaspoon ground nutmeg

$\frac{1}{8}$ teaspoon salt

$\frac{1}{8}$ teaspoon ground black pepper

1 small tomato, chopped

$\frac{1}{2}$ cup grated Cheddar cheese, divided

4 slices whole-wheat French bread, toasted

1. Heat 2 tablespoons olive oil in a medium frying pan over medium-low heat. Add mushrooms and onion. Cook until onion is tender. Remove from pan and set aside. Clean the pan.

2. In a medium bowl, lightly beat the eggs with the milk. Stir in nutmeg, salt, and pepper. Stir in cooked mushrooms and onion, tomato, and $\frac{1}{4}$ cup grated cheese.

3. Heat remaining 2 tablespoons olive oil in the frying pan on medium-low heat. Swirl the oil around the pan to coat the pan entirely. Pour the egg mixture into the pan. Move the vegetables around if necessary to make sure they are evenly mixed throughout the egg. Cook the frittata over medium-low heat. Tilt the pan occasionally or lift edges of the frittata with a spatula so that the uncooked egg runs underneath.

CHEESE AND
MUSHROOM FRITTATA CONT.

4. When the frittata is firm on top, cover the frying pan with a lid or plate. Turn the pan over so that the frittata falls onto the lid. Return the pan to the stovetop and slide the frittata back into the pan, so that the bottom of the frittata is on top.

5. Sprinkle remaining $1/4$ cup grated cheese over the frittata. Cook over medium-low heat until the cheese is melted and the frittata is cooked through. To serve, cut the frittata pizza-style into wedges and serve on top of the toasted French bread.

PER SERVING
Calories: 339 — Fat: 22g — Sodium: 361mg — Fiber: 3g
Carbohydrates: 18g — Sugar: 5g — Protein: 14g

HERB-STUFFED TOMATOES WITH FETA

SERVES 2

Adopting a plant-based diet is all about thinking outside the box. In other words, breakfast doesn't have to mean bacon and eggs. Serve these stuffed tomatoes with whole-wheat toast. If you don't have a slow cooker, consider investing in one—they are easy to use and impart deep flavors to food.

INGREDIENTS

2 large tomatoes

I ounce feta cheese, crumbled

I medium stalk celery, minced

I tablespoon minced fresh garlic

2 tablespoons minced fresh oregano

2 tablespoons minced fresh Italian parsley

I teaspoon dried chervil

I teaspoon fennel seeds

¾ cup water

1. Cut out the core of each tomato and discard. Scoop the seeds out of the tomatoes, leaving the walls intact.

2. In a small bowl, stir together feta, celery, garlic, herbs, and fennel seeds. Divide into two even portions, and stuff one portion into the center of each tomato.

3. Place filled tomatoes in a 4-quart slow cooker. Pour water into the bottom of the slow cooker. Cook on low for 4 hours.

PER SERVING

Calories: 86 – Fat: 3g – Sodium: 156mg – Fiber: 4g

Carbohydrates: 12g – Sugar: 5g – Protein: 4g

How to Choose Feta Cheese

When choosing a feta cheese, check the ingredients list to be sure it is organic and comes from goat or sheep's milk rather than cow's milk.

SPINACH AND RICOTTA MINI QUICHES

SERVES 6

Breakfast for the week (assuming your roommates don't eat it all)! Top these mini quiches with a slice of tomato and sprinkle on some shredded cheese to add a nice touch of color and great flavor.

INGREDIENTS

- 1 (10-ounce) package chopped frozen spinach
- 2 large eggs
- 1 cup part-skim ricotta cheese
- 1 cup shredded low-fat mozzarella cheese

1. Preheat oven to 350°F. Grease a twelve-hole muffin tin or line with paper muffin cups.

2. Heat spinach in microwave according to package directions, until soft and warm.

3. In a medium bowl, whip eggs and add spinach. Blend together. Fold in ricotta and mozzarella.

4. Fill each cup (about $1/2$" deep) with the egg and spinach mixture. Bake 30–35 minutes.

PER SERVING (2 MINI QUICHES)
Calories: 332 – Fat: 20g – Sodium: 443mg – Fiber: 3g
Carbohydrates: 9g – Sugar: 2g – Protein: 26g

VANILLA FLAX GRANOLA
MAKES 2½ CUPS

Serve this granola on top of Greek yogurt with berries, with almond milk as a cereal, or in a plastic baggie in the back of the classroom! To add a subtle nutty flavor and up your omega-3 fatty acids for the day, add whole flaxseeds.

INGREDIENTS

⅓ cup maple syrup

⅓ cup coconut oil

1½ teaspoons vanilla extract

2 cups rolled oats (not the quick-cooking kind)

½ cup flaxseed meal

¾ cup dried fruit, diced

1. Preheat oven to 325°F.

2. In a medium saucepan, melt and whisk together maple syrup, coconut oil, and vanilla over low heat until oil is melted.

3. Toss together oats, flaxseed meal, and dried fruit on a large baking tray in a single layer (you may need to use two trays).

4. Drizzle the maple syrup mixture over oats and fruit, gently tossing to combine as needed.

5. Bake for 25–30 minutes, carefully tossing once during cooking. Granola will harden as it cools.

PER SERVING (¼ CUP)
Calories: 223 — Fat: 10g — Sodium: 1mg — Fiber: 4g
Carbohydrates: 29g — Sugar: 13g — Protein: 4g

SAVORY SCRAMBLED EGGS
SERVES 1

If you choose a refined carbohydrate for breakfast, but don't pair it with a protein, your body will crave quick sources of energy from carbs throughout the rest of the day, creating a roller-coaster effect on your mood. Eggs are packed with stomach-filling protein, which can help reduce your appetite throughout the day.

INGREDIENTS

2 large eggs

2 tablespoons whole milk

$\frac{1}{8}$ teaspoon salt

$\frac{1}{8}$ teaspoon ground black pepper

10 capers

2 tablespoons unsalted butter, divided

$\frac{1}{2}$ medium tomato, chopped

1 small green onion, chopped

1. Break eggs into a small bowl. Add milk, salt, pepper, and capers. Beat until the eggs are an even color throughout.

2. In a small frying pan, melt 1 tablespoon butter on low heat.

3. Add tomato and green onion to the pan. Cook until tomato is tender but still firm. Remove from pan and set aside. Clean the pan.

4. Melt remaining 1 tablespoon butter in the pan on low heat.

5. Turn the heat up to medium-low and add the eggs to the pan. Cook eggs, using a spatula to turn sections of the egg from time to time so that the uncooked egg on top flows underneath. Adjust the heat up or down as needed.

6. When eggs are nearly cooked, return tomato and green onion to pan. Cook until eggs are firm but still a bit moist (about 6–8 minutes).

PER SERVING

Calories: 380 — Fat: 31g — Sodium: 653mg — Fiber: 1g

Carbohydrates: 6g — Sugar: 4g — Protein: 15g

PEAR AND PUMPKIN BREAKFAST BREAD

SERVES 16

This bread is delicious served as is for breakfast, or try it in your favorite French toast recipe. Using a different combination of puréed fruits and vegetables instead of the pears and pumpkin will make a more interesting final product.

INGREDIENTS

$\frac{1}{2}$ cup canned pumpkin purée

$\frac{1}{2}$ cup canned puréed pears

2 large eggs

$\frac{3}{4}$ cup maple syrup

$\frac{1}{4}$ cup canned full-fat coconut milk

1 teaspoon vanilla extract

1 cup almond flour

$\frac{3}{4}$ cup coconut flour

2 tablespoons arrowroot powder

$\frac{1}{2}$ teaspoon salt

$\frac{1}{8}$ teaspoon baking soda

$\frac{1}{4}$ teaspoon cream of tartar

$\frac{1}{2}$ teaspoon ground cinnamon

$\frac{1}{4}$ teaspoon ground nutmeg

$\frac{1}{4}$ teaspoon ground cardamom

1. Preheat oven to 350°F. Line a 9" × 5" loaf pan with parchment paper and set aside.

2. In a large bowl, combine pumpkin, pears, eggs, maple syrup, coconut milk, and vanilla and beat well.

3. In a medium bowl, stir together almond flour, coconut flour, arrowroot powder, salt, baking soda, cream of tartar, cinnamon, nutmeg, and cardamom.

4. Add the dry ingredients to the pumpkin mixture and mix well. Pour into prepared loaf pan.

5. Bake for 40–50 minutes or until a toothpick inserted in the center comes out clean. Cool in pan for 15 minutes, then remove loaf and move to a wire rack to cool completely.

PER SERVING

Calories: 131 — Fat: 6g — Sodium: 97mg — Fiber: 3g
Carbohydrates: 17g — Sugar: 11g — Protein: 4g

TOASTED NUT "CEREAL"
MAKES 10 CUPS

Cereal is a college breakfast staple. But packaged products are loaded with sweeteners, preservatives, and artificial colors. Instead, try making your own "cereal" and you won't miss the packaged stuff at all.

INGREDIENTS

1 1/2 cups pumpkin seeds

1 cup sunflower seeds

1 1/2 cups sliced almonds

1 1/2 cups chopped pecans

1 1/2 cups unsweetened shredded coconut

1/3 cup maple syrup

1/3 cup coconut oil

1 teaspoon ground cinnamon

2 teaspoons vanilla extract

1 cup dried cranberries

1 cup chopped dried apricots

1 cup golden raisins

1. Preheat oven to 375°F. Line a large rimmed baking sheet with parchment paper and set aside.

2. In a large bowl, combine pumpkin seeds, sunflower seeds, almonds, pecans, and coconut. Spread the mixture onto the lined baking sheet.

3. In a small saucepan, combine maple syrup and coconut oil and heat gently until oil is melted. Remove from heat and stir in cinnamon and vanilla. Drizzle over the mixture on baking sheet and toss to coat. Spread evenly.

4. Bake for 20–30 minutes, stirring every 10 minutes, until light golden brown and fragrant. Remove from oven and stir in cranberries, apricots, and raisins. Let stand until cool, stirring occasionally. Store in an airtight container at room temperature for up to a few weeks.

PER SERVING (1 CUP)
Calories: 609 – Fat: 41g – Sodium: 6mg – Fiber: 11g
Carbohydrates: 55g – Sugar: 33g – Protein: 10g

VERY VEGGIE OMELET
SERVES 2

The dining hall's omelet can't compare! Vary this recipe by chopping up any vegetable you like and adding it or substituting it for the peppers. If you like a little spice, try a dash of Tabasco sauce to kick up the flavor.

INGREDIENTS

6 large egg whites

2 large whole eggs

$\frac{1}{4}$ teaspoon salt

$\frac{1}{2}$ cup chopped red bell pepper

$\frac{1}{2}$ cup chopped green bell pepper

$\frac{1}{4}$ cup chopped yellow onion

$\frac{1}{2}$ cup chopped button mushrooms

1 tablespoon olive oil

1. In a small bowl, beat egg whites and whole eggs together. Mix in salt.

2. In a medium bowl, combine bell peppers, onions, and mushrooms.

3. In a small skillet over low heat, warm the olive oil.

4. Pour the egg mixture into the skillet to coat the surface. Cook until edges show firmness.

5. Add the vegetable mixture so that it covers the entire egg mixture evenly. Fold one side over the other to form a half-moon shape.

6. Flip the omelet and cook on the second side until desired doneness is reached.

PER SERVING
Calories: 21 – Fat: 11g – Sodium: 528mg – Fiber: 2g
Carbohydrates: 8g – Sugar: 5g – Protein: 19g

SWEET POTATO HASH BROWNS WITH SCRAMBLED EGGS

SERVES 6

These Sweet Potato Hash Browns with Scrambled Eggs are likely to become a favorite among your roommates. While hash is typically served with meat, this recipe showcases the flavorful sweet potatoes; it's a good example of how a plant-based diet doesn't have to mean deprivation. Loading up on all the protein in this dish will ensure you have enough energy to get through your morning classes.

INGREDIENTS

2 tablespoons coconut oil

3 medium sweet potatoes, peeled and grated

1 tablespoon unsalted butter

6 large eggs

$\frac{1}{4}$ teaspoon salt

$\frac{1}{8}$ teaspoon ground black pepper

1. Heat coconut oil in a large skillet over medium-high heat. Cook sweet potatoes in hot oil for 7 minutes, stirring often. Drain on paper towels.

2. Meanwhile, in a medium skillet, heat butter over medium heat. Pour in eggs and cook until no visible liquid egg remains, stirring occasionally. Season with salt and pepper.

3. To serve, top the hash browns with the cooked eggs.

PER SERVING

Calories: 178 — Fat: 10g — Sodium: 188mg — Fiber: 2g
Carbohydrates: 12g — Sugar: 4g — Protein: 7g

LOADED WHITE BEAN AVOCADO TOAST
SERVES 2

You've likely seen avocado toast all over social media and may have been tempted to make it as a breakfast of your own. This recipe gives your toast a protein-filled boost by mixing in some white beans with the avocado. You can barely taste the beans, but they'll make your meal more nutritious and filling.

INGREDIENTS

2 thin slices multigrain sourdough bread

$3/4$ cup canned cannellini beans, drained and rinsed

1 medium ripe avocado, peeled and pitted

3 tablespoons fresh lemon juice

$1/4$ cup assorted microgreens

2 tablespoons hemp seeds

$1/2$ teaspoon red pepper flakes

1. Toast bread until golden and crispy.

2. Add beans to a medium bowl and mash with a fork to make a paste. Add avocado and mash with a fork, folding avocado chunks into beans. Mix in lemon juice.

3. Spread the mixture evenly on the toast, and top with microgreens, hemp seeds, and red pepper flakes. Serve immediately.

PER SERVING
Calories: 289 – Fat: 15g – Sodium: 209mg – Fiber: 12g
Carbohydrates: 30g – Sugar: 1g – Protein: 12g

Hemp Seeds
Student athletes may want to check with their coaches for guidance before using hemp seeds. Some athletes who consume hemp seeds may be at risk for a positive anti-doping test, and some schools ban hemp seeds altogether.

SAVORY BREAKFAST QUINOA BOWL
SERVES 2

Quinoa doesn't have to be just for lunch or dinner—it's an excellent protein source that can be eaten for breakfast as well. In this recipe, quinoa is mixed with tofu and spinach and topped off with avocado, sun-dried tomatoes, and feta cheese. All these amazing flavors combine to give you a perfect plant-based energy boost before a long morning lecture.

INGREDIENTS

$\frac{1}{2}$ cup uncooked quinoa, rinsed well and drained

1 cup water

8 ounces firm organic tofu

1 tablespoon olive oil

3 cups fresh spinach leaves

$\frac{1}{2}$ medium ripe avocado, peeled, pitted, and diced

$\frac{1}{3}$ cup chopped oil-packed sun-dried tomatoes

2 tablespoons crumbled feta cheese

2 tablespoons fresh lemon juice

$\frac{1}{4}$ teaspoon ground black pepper

1. Add quinoa and water to a medium saucepan; bring to a boil over medium-high heat. Reduce to a simmer, cover, and cook until all water is absorbed, about 10–15 minutes.

2. Drain tofu and pat dry with paper towels. Add to a small bowl and mash with a fork until crumbly; set aside. Heat oil in a large saucepan over medium heat. Add spinach and sauté about 2 minutes until wilted. Lower heat to medium-low and add tofu. Cook about 1 minute until heated through. Mix in quinoa.

3. Transfer to a medium bowl and top with avocado, tomatoes, feta, lemon juice, and pepper. Serve warm.

PER SERVING
Calories: 428 – Fat: 22g – Sodium: 187mg – Fiber: 8g
Carbohydrates: 40g – Sugar: 2g – Protein: 20g

VEGETABLE TOFU SCRAMBLE
SERVES 2

In this recipe, mashed tofu is a great substitution for scrambled eggs. It has a similar texture and consistency, and it's just as filling. Load it up with all your favorite toppings and make this dish your own.

INGREDIENTS

8 ounces organic extra-firm tofu

1 tablespoon olive oil

2 medium cloves garlic, peeled and finely chopped

1/2 cup chopped yellow onion

1 1/4 cups sliced button mushrooms

2 cups fresh baby spinach leaves

1/2 cup quartered cherry tomatoes

1/2 teaspoon turmeric powder

1/4 teaspoon salt

1/2 teaspoon ground black pepper

1. Drain all liquid from tofu and place between paper towels to soak up any excess moisture. Let it sit about 5 minutes, then transfer to a medium bowl. Break up with a fork until crumbled.

2. Heat oil in a medium skillet over medium-low heat. Add garlic and cook 1 minute, stirring so it doesn't burn. Add onions and mushrooms; cook 4–5 minutes until onions are translucent and mushrooms begin to soften, stirring occasionally. Add spinach and cook about 2 minutes or until spinach begins to wilt.

3. Add cherry tomatoes, tofu, and turmeric; stir about 1 minute until tofu is heated through and all ingredients are evenly mixed. Season with salt and pepper. Serve warm.

PER SERVING
Calories: 208 – Fat: 13g – Sodium: 328mg – Fiber: 3g
Carbohydrates: 12g – Sugar: 4g – Protein: 15g

Always Opt for Organic Tofu
More than 90 percent of soy is genetically modified, so whenever you buy tofu, make sure to get organic. Research is mixed on GMOs, but better safe than sorry!

SAVORY CHICKPEA OATMEAL WITH GARLIC YOGURT SAUCE

SERVES 2

When most people think of oatmeal, they think sweet, but just like any other grain, oatmeal can be prepared as a savory dish as well. The roasted chickpeas in this dish provide a hit of extra plant-based protein, and the soft sweetness of the tomatoes balances out the crispness of the chickpeas.

INGREDIENTS

1 cup canned chickpeas, drained and rinsed

1 cup halved cherry tomatoes

1 tablespoon plus 1 teaspoon olive oil, divided

1 cup steel-cut oats

½ cup 2% plain Greek yogurt

¼ teaspoon garlic powder

¼ teaspoon paprika

½ small ripe avocado, peeled, pitted, and sliced

⅛ teaspoon salt

¼ teaspoon ground black pepper

1. Preheat oven to 425°F.

2. Pat chickpeas dry with a paper towel (removing the excess moisture before baking will help make them crispy). Line a medium baking sheet with aluminum foil.

3. Spread out chickpeas and tomatoes evenly on the prepared baking sheet; drizzle with 1 tablespoon oil. Bake 20 minutes until chickpeas are golden and crispy.

4. While chickpeas and tomatoes are roasting, prepare oats according to package directions.

5. In a small bowl, combine yogurt, garlic powder, and paprika until smooth.

6. When oats are ready, add to a medium serving bowl and top with roasted chickpeas and tomatoes, avocado slices, prepared yogurt sauce, remaining 1 teaspoon olive oil, salt, and pepper. Serve warm.

PER SERVING

Calories: 628 — Fat: 21g — Sodium: 332mg — Fiber: 18g
Carbohydrates: 84g — Sugar: 7g — Protein: 26g

KALE, SWEET POTATO, AND TEMPEH BREAKFAST HASH
SERVES 3

Skip the boring breakfast hash with eggs that your dining hall mass-produces. For a plant-based alternative, you can use tempeh, which not only provides a good source of protein but also helps make the dish heartier.

INGREDIENTS

1 medium unpeeled sweet potato, diced

2 tablespoons olive oil, divided

2 medium cloves garlic, peeled and finely chopped

1/2 medium yellow onion, peeled and chopped

3 cups chopped fresh kale

1/2 cup crumbled tempeh

2 tablespoons apple cider vinegar

1/2 teaspoon paprika

1/2 teaspoon cayenne pepper

2 tablespoons nutritional yeast

1/4 teaspoon ground black pepper

1. Preheat oven to 425°F. Line a 10" × 15" baking sheet with aluminum foil.

2. Add potatoes and 1 tablespoon oil to a small bowl; toss until evenly coated. Spread potatoes on the prepared baking sheet and bake 20 minutes until potatoes are soft but crispy on the outside.

3. Heat remaining 1 tablespoon oil in a large skillet over medium-low heat. Add garlic and cook 1 minute, stirring so garlic doesn't burn. Add onions and sauté 3 minutes. Add kale and sauté 2 minutes or until it begins to wilt. Add tempeh and cook 1 more minute.

4. Add sweet potatoes to skillet along with vinegar, paprika, cayenne pepper, and yeast. Cook about 1–2 minutes, stirring constantly until well mixed and heated through. Top with black pepper and serve warm.

PER SERVING
Calories: 201 — Fat: 12g — Sodium: 37mg — Fiber: 3g

Carbohydrates: 17g — Sugar: 3g — Protein: 8g

TOFU BREAKFAST BURRITO
MAKES 2 BURRITOS

This recipe is totally vegan because it uses vegan cheese, a substitute for dairy cheese that is most commonly made from soy as well as other ingredients such as rice and nuts. Many soy cheeses have calcium added, which means you still get the benefits of dairy cheese. Serve with hot sauce for an extra kick!

INGREDIENTS

1 (14-ounce) block firm or extra-firm organic tofu

2 tablespoons olive oil

$\frac{1}{2}$ cup salsa

$\frac{1}{2}$ teaspoon chili powder

$\frac{1}{8}$ teaspoon salt

$\frac{1}{8}$ teaspoon ground black pepper

2 (6") whole-wheat tortillas, warmed

2 teaspoons hot sauce

2 slices vegan cheese

$\frac{1}{2}$ medium ripe avocado, peeled, pitted, and sliced

1. Drain all liquid from tofu and place between paper towels to soak up any excess moisture, then cube or crumble tofu into 1" chunks. In a small skillet over medium heat, sauté tofu in olive oil 2–3 minutes.

2. Add salsa and chili powder and cook 2–3 minutes more, stirring frequently. Season with salt and pepper.

3. Layer each tortilla with half of the tofu and salsa mixture and drizzle each with 1 teaspoon hot sauce.

4. Add a slice of cheese and half of the avocado slices to each tortilla and wrap like a burrito. Serve.

PER SERVING (1 BURRITO)
Calories: 493 – Fat: 31g – Sodium: 1,162mg – Fiber: 10g
Carbohydrates: 35g – Sugar: 6g – Protein: 22g

VEGAN PANCAKES
MAKES 10 PANCAKES

A touch of sugar and hint of sweet banana flavor more than makes up for the lack of eggs and butter in this pancake recipe. Serve with pure maple syrup—not the kind that's mixed with sugar or corn syrup, so you're not adding anything but extra sweetness to your dish.

INGREDIENTS

1 cup all-purpose flour

1 tablespoon vegan sugar

1¾ teaspoons baking powder

¼ teaspoon salt

½ medium banana, peeled

1 teaspoon vanilla extract

1 cup soy milk

1. In a large bowl, mix together flour, sugar, baking powder, and salt.

2. In a small bowl, mash banana with a fork. Add vanilla extract and whisk until smooth and fluffy. Add soy milk and stir to combine well.

3. Add the soy milk mixture to the flour and dry ingredients, stirring just until combined.

4. Heat a lightly greased griddle or large frying pan over medium heat. Drop batter about 3 tablespoons at a time and heat until bubbles appear on surface, 2–3 minutes. Flip and cook other side until lightly golden brown, another 1–2 minutes. Serve.

PER SERVING (1 PANCAKE)
Calories: 78 — Fat: 0g — Sodium: 152mg — Fiber: 1g
Carbohydrates: 13g — Sugar: 3g — Protein: 2g

Don't Overmix!

When it comes to mixing pancake batter, less is more! Pancakes should be light and fluffy, but overmixing the batter will make them tough and rubbery. Gently combine the wet ingredients with the dry ones and don't be afraid of a few lumps; they'll sort themselves out when heated. If you let the batter sit for about 5 minutes, you'll need to stir even less.

BREAKFAST TACOS
MAKES 4 TACOS

Breakfast tacos are a fun and unique breakfast, whether you're serving them for brunch or just making them for yourself on a regular morning. Instead of eggs, these tacos are made with a tofu scramble and filled with black beans and spinach for an extra dose of plant-based protein.

INGREDIENTS

4 (6") corn tortillas

1½ tablespoons olive oil, divided

2 medium cloves garlic, peeled and minced

4 cups fresh spinach leaves

8 ounces extra-firm organic tofu

½ teaspoon ground cumin

1 teaspoon chili powder

¼ teaspoon salt

1½ cups canned black beans, drained and rinsed

8 cherry tomatoes, halved

1 large ripe avocado, peeled, pitted, and sliced

2 tablespoons fresh lime juice

1. Place tortillas on serving plates. In a large pan, heat 1 tablespoon olive oil on medium-low. Add garlic and cook 1 minute. Add spinach and cook 2–3 minutes until wilted. Spoon the spinach on top of the tortillas, dividing it evenly among them.

2. Drain tofu and pat dry with a paper towel. Add to a small bowl and mash with a fork.

3. In the same pan that you used for the spinach, heat remaining ½ tablespoon oil on medium-low. Add tofu, cumin, chili powder, and salt. Mix with a spatula, and cook 1–2 minutes until tofu is evenly coated and warm. Add the tofu to the tortillas on top of the spinach, dividing it evenly among them.

4. Add black beans to the same pan and cook 1–2 minutes until warm. Add the beans to the tacos, dividing them evenly.

5. Top tacos with equal amounts tomatoes, avocado, and lime juice and serve immediately.

PER SERVING (1 TACO)
Calories: 306 — Fat: 14g — Sodium: 411mg — Fiber: 12g
Carbohydrates: 34g — Sugar: 2g — Protein: 14g

PUMPKIN PIE CHIA SEED PUDDING

SERVES 4

Nutrient-dense chia seeds are a great plant-based protein source. You can sprinkle them on lots of foods, or use them to make this pudding-like breakfast (or any time!) treat. This pudding is inspired by the flavors of fall and pumpkin pie, but as long as you have canned pumpkin, you can make it all year long.

INGREDIENTS

1 1/2 cups unsweetened almond milk

1/2 cup canned pumpkin purée

1 teaspoon vanilla extract

1 teaspoon pumpkin pie spice

1/3 cup chia seeds

1 teaspoon maple syrup

1/4 teaspoon ground cinnamon

1/4 cup chopped pecans

1. In a blender or food processor, blend together almond milk, pumpkin purée, vanilla, and pumpkin spice on high until creamy, about 10 seconds.

2. Add chia seeds and do quick little pulses to mix seeds into the liquid. You don't want to blend up the chia seeds, just evenly disperse them.

3. Place the mixture into a pint-sized jar or medium bowl, cover, and place in the refrigerator. Let sit overnight or until the pudding is thick in texture. Top with maple syrup, cinnamon, and pecans before serving.

PER SERVING

Calories: 145 – Fat: 10g – Sodium: 70mg – Fiber: 7g

Carbohydrates: 12g – Sugar: 3g – Protein: 4g

PEANUT BUTTER CUP OATMEAL
SERVES 1

This creamy combination of chocolate and peanut butter tastes like it should be dessert, but it doesn't include any refined sugar! It's loaded with plant-based fiber and protein to get you through a long day of classes.

INGREDIENTS

$\frac{1}{2}$ cup water

$\frac{1}{2}$ cup unsweetened almond milk

$\frac{1}{2}$ cup rolled oats

2 tablespoons creamy peanut butter

1 tablespoon unsweetened cocoa powder

1 $\frac{1}{2}$ teaspoons maple syrup

1. Add water and almond milk to a medium saucepan and bring to a boil over medium-high heat. Add oats and reduce to a simmer. Cover and cook 3–5 minutes until oats are soft.

2. Remove from heat and mix in peanut butter, cocoa powder, and maple syrup until evenly combined. Serve warm.

PER SERVING

Calories: 433 — Fat: 21g — Sodium: 97mg — Fiber: 9g

Carbohydrates: 50g — Sugar: 11g — Protein: 16g

BANANA HONEY PANCAKES
SERVES 4

These protein-filled banana pancakes don't contain any dairy, and the only sweetener used is honey. To get an extra protein boost, you can top them with walnuts, chia seeds, almond butter, or anything else that will help you start off your morning on the right foot.

INGREDIENTS

1 medium ripe banana,
    peeled and mashed

1 cup unsweetened almond milk

1 teaspoon vanilla extract

$\frac{1}{4}$ cup honey

1 cup whole-wheat flour

$\frac{1}{2}$ cup DIY Protein Powder
    (see recipe in Chapter 8)

$\frac{1}{4}$ teaspoon ground cinnamon

1 $\frac{1}{2}$ teaspoons baking powder

1 $\frac{1}{2}$ tablespoons coconut oil, divided

1. In a large bowl, combine banana, almond milk, vanilla, and honey until smooth.

2. In a medium bowl, combine flour, DIY Protein Powder, cinnamon, and baking powder. Fold the dry ingredients into the wet ingredients until just combined (don't overmix to ensure your pancakes come out light and fluffy).

3. In a large skillet, heat $\frac{1}{2}$ tablespoon coconut oil on medium. Add the batter to the pan using about $\frac{1}{4}$ cup of batter per pancake. Cook about 2–3 minutes on each side, flipping when bubbly on top and the edges begin to firm up. Repeat until all batter is gone and you've made eight medium pancakes, adding coconut oil to the pan as needed. Serve warm.

PER SERVING (2 PANCAKES)
Calories: 391 – Fat: 17g – Sodium: 230mg – Fiber: 9g
Carbohydrates: 54g – Sugar: 21g – Protein: 11g

RASPBERRY BREAKFAST BARS
MAKES 9 BARS

These fruity breakfast bars are perfect to grab when you're running late for class. They're low in sugar, as they're mostly sweetened by the fruit, with just a wee bit of coconut sugar added. They'll give you all the protein and carbohydrates you need to start your day with energy.

INGREDIENTS

2 tablespoons flaxseed meal

6 tablespoons warm water

1 1/2 cups rolled oats

1 cup almond flour

1 teaspoon baking powder

1/4 cup hemp seeds

1/4 cup chia seeds

2 tablespoons coconut sugar

1 large ripe banana, peeled and mashed

1/4 cup crunchy almond butter

1 teaspoon vanilla extract

1/4 cup unsweetened almond milk

1 cup fresh raspberries

1. Preheat oven to 350°F. Line an 8" × 8" baking pan with parchment paper and grease the sides with cooking spray.

2. In a small bowl, combine flaxseed meal and warm water to create a "flax egg." Stir and let sit 15 minutes until flaxseeds are gummy.

3. In a large bowl, mix together oats, almond flour, baking powder, hemp seeds, chia seeds, and coconut sugar.

4. In a medium bowl, mix together banana, almond butter, vanilla, and flaxseed egg. Pour this mixture into the large bowl, and mix well. Mix in almond milk and raspberries. Don't worry if the raspberries get crushed in the process.

5. Pour the batter into the prepared baking pan and smooth the top with a spoon. Bake 30–35 minutes until edges begin to get crisp and top is golden and firm. Let cool 15 minutes, and then cut into squares.

PER SERVING (1 BAR)
Calories: 226 – Fat: 15g – Sodium: 77mg – Fiber: 7g
Carbohydrates: 25g – Sugar: 7g – Protein: 9g

CHAPTER 3
SNACKS

Spicy Jalapeño Poppers 50

Peanutty Bananas............................ 51

Vegan Spinach and Artichoke Dip ... 52

Fresh Mint Spring Rolls...................... 53

Vegetable Kebabs............................ 54

Curried Kale Chips............................ 55

Homemade Trail Mix......................... 56

Roasted Parsnip Chips...................... 57

No-Bake Tex-Mex Nachos 58

Chocolate Nut Bars 60

Italian Pesto Popcorn......................... 61

Roasted Pistachios 62

Graham Crackers 63

Veggie-Packed Potato Skins 64

Ginger Vegetable Spring Rolls 65

Spicy White Bean Citrus Dip 66

Roasted Cashew and
Spicy Basil Pesto............................... 67

Chewy Granola Bars........................... 69

Tomato and Dill–Stuffed
Grape Leaves (Dolmas)..................... 70

Fried Zucchini Sticks 71

Vegan Tzatziki..................................... 72

Avocado and Shiitake Pot Stickers.... 73

Chili Cheese Dip.................................. 74

Simple Scallion Pancakes 75

Mexican Loaded French Fries............ 76

Trail Mix Crunch 77

SPICY JALAPEÑO POPPERS
SERVES 12

You can experiment with this recipe by stuffing the poppers with different cheeses. Use feta to make the poppers more Mediterranean-inspired or goat cheese to make the poppers creamier. Just be sure to wear gloves while cutting the peppers and scooping out the seeds to protect your hands from the spicy juices!

INGREDIENTS

1 cup vegan yogurt

$\frac{1}{2}$ medium red onion, peeled and minced

$\frac{1}{2}$ cup minced tomatoes

2 tablespoons minced fresh garlic

1 teaspoon salt

12 medium jalapeño peppers

1 cup almond milk

1 cup whole-wheat flour

$\frac{1}{2}$ cup olive oil

1. In a medium bowl, combine yogurt, onion, tomatoes, garlic, and salt.

2. Remove tops and seeds from jalapeños, then stuff with the yogurt mixture.

3. Pour almond milk into a shallow dish, and fill another shallow dish with whole-wheat flour.

4. Dip each jalapeño into the almond milk and roll in the flour; set aside.

5. Heat oil in a large skillet over medium heat. Add the jalapeños and cook until golden brown all over, turning regularly.

6. Remove Spicy Jalapeño Poppers from skillet and place onto paper towels to soak up excess oil.

PER SERVING
Calories: 89 – Fat: 6g – Sodium: 201mg – Fiber: 1g
Carbohydrates: 8g – Sugar: 2g – Protein: 2g

PEANUTTY BANANAS
SERVES 4

Your reward after a long study session! Try this recipe with almond or cashew butter for variation. Honey may also be substituted for the brown rice syrup.

INGREDIENTS

3 medium bananas

1 cup crunchy peanut butter

$\frac{1}{4}$ cup brown rice syrup

1 cup granola

1. Peel bananas and cut them into quarters crosswise.

2. Stand the banana pieces cut-sides up on a platter. (Cut the pointed tips off the end pieces so they can stand up.)

3. Mix the peanut butter with the brown rice syrup in a medium glass bowl and microwave on high for 15–20 seconds. Stir together well.

4. Spoon the peanut butter mixture onto the banana pieces.

5. Sprinkle granola over the peanut butter and serve.

PER SERVING
Calories: 682 – Fat: 36g – Sodium: 54mg – Fiber: 10g
Carbohydrates: 68g – Sugar: 33g – Protein: 21g

VEGAN SPINACH AND ARTICHOKE DIP

MAKES 4 CUPS

Spinach and artichoke dip is usually viewed as an indulgent, unhealthy splurge, but this version is not only healthy; it's also rich in protein. It might seem hard to believe, but there's no cream or cheese in this version. Serve with toasted pita points or slices of warm French bread and you'll be the hero of your study group.

INGREDIENTS

1 (15-ounce) can artichokes, drained and chopped

2 cups water

1 teaspoon lemon juice

1 tablespoon vegan margarine

1 cup thawed chopped frozen spinach

8 ounces vegan cream cheese

16 ounces vegan sour cream

$\frac{1}{3}$ cup vegan Parmesan cheese

$\frac{1}{4}$ teaspoon garlic powder

$\frac{1}{4}$ teaspoon salt

1. In a 4-quart slow cooker, add all ingredients.

2. Cover and cook over low heat 1 hour.

PER SERVING (1 CUP)

Calories: 452 – Fat: 37g – Sodium: 1,050mg – Fiber: 12g
Carbohydrates: 31g – Sugar: 1g – Protein: 7g

Serving Options

This recipe calls for serving the dip warm, but chilling the dip and serving it cool is also delicious. After cooking, let the dip cool to room temperature and store in the refrigerator in an airtight container. Let cool at least 3 hours before serving.

FRESH MINT SPRING ROLLS
SERVES 3

Wrapping spring rolls is a balance between getting them tight enough to hold together, but not so tight the thin wrappers break! It's like riding a bike: Once you've got it, you've got it, and then spring rolls can be very quick and fun to make.

INGREDIENTS

1 (3-ounce) package clear bean thread noodles

1 cup hot water

1 tablespoon soy sauce

$\frac{1}{2}$ teaspoon ground ginger

1 teaspoon sesame oil

$\frac{1}{4}$ cup diced shiitake mushrooms

1 medium carrot, peeled and grated

12 (8$\frac{1}{2}$") spring roll wrappers

Warm water

$\frac{1}{2}$ medium head green leaf lettuce, chopped

1 medium cucumber, peeled and sliced thin

1 cup fresh mint

1. Break noodles in half to make smaller pieces, then submerge in 1 cup hot water until soft, 6–7 minutes. Drain.

2. In a large bowl, toss together the hot noodles with the soy sauce, ginger, sesame oil, mushrooms, and carrots, tossing well to combine.

3. In a large shallow pan, carefully submerge spring roll wrappers one at a time in warm water until just barely soft. Remove from water and place a bit of lettuce in the center of the wrapper. Add about 2 tablespoons of the noodle mixture, a few slices of cucumber, and place three mint leaves on top.

4. Fold the bottom of the wrapper over the filling, fold in each side, then roll.

PER SERVING
Calories: 302 – Fat: 2g – Sodium: 482mg – Fiber: 3g
Carbohydrates: 68g – Sugar: 5g – Protein: 5g

To Dip or Not to Dip
Store-bought sweet chili sauce, spicy sriracha sauce, or a Japanese salad dressing or marinade will work in a pinch, but a simple homemade dip is best for these spring rolls. Experiment with soy sauce, rice vinegar, sesame oil, and a dash of red pepper flakes.

VEGETABLE KEBABS
SERVES 6

Serve these kebabs as an appetizer at parties so your guests can easily handle the food without using cutlery. This colorful treat won't leave you missing the processed party foods.

INGREDIENTS

6 wooden skewers, cut in half and soaked in water for at least 1 hour

12 small green onions, trimmed

1 large red bell pepper, seeded and cut into large chunks

1 large yellow bell pepper, seeded and cut into large chunks

1 large green bell pepper, seeded and cut into large chunks

12 large button mushrooms

1 tablespoon olive oil

$\frac{1}{2}$ tablespoon ground black pepper

1. Preheat grill or broiler.

2. Thread vegetables onto skewers, and brush all sides of vegetables with oil. Season with pepper.

3. Place skewers on the grill or under the broiler, paying close attention as they cook, as they can easily burn. Cook about 10 minutes, until vegetables are fork-tender.

PER SERVING
Calories: 62 – Fat: 2g – Sodium: 9mg – Fiber: 3g
Carbohydrates: 9g – Sugar: 3g – Protein: 3g

Soaking the Skewers
When using wooden skewers, always soak them in water for an hour before spearing the food items. Soaking the skewers allows you to place them on the grill for a time without them burning.

CURRIED KALE CHIPS
SERVES 6

If you're feeling tempted by processed potato chips after a long day of classes, try these chips instead! The kale and curry powder combo is not only healthy—it tastes wonderful too. You might never go back to the vending machines!

INGREDIENTS

14 ounces fresh kale

2 tablespoons olive oil

1 tablespoon melted coconut oil

2 tablespoons curry powder

1 teaspoon ground ginger

$\frac{1}{2}$ teaspoon ground cardamom

$\frac{1}{4}$ teaspoon cayenne pepper

1 teaspoon salt

1. Preheat oven to 350°F. Wash kale well and dry thoroughly. Cut out any large ribs and discard. Cut kale leaves into 3" pieces.

2. In a small bowl, combine olive oil and coconut oil and mix well. Stir in curry powder, ginger, cardamom, and cayenne pepper and mix until combined.

3. Pour the curry mixture over kale leaves and massage with your hands until the leaves are coated. Arrange leaves in a single layer on two large baking sheets. Bake for 15–18 minutes, rotating pans after 10 minutes. The kale will not be crisp.

4. Remove from oven and sprinkle with salt. Let stand until leaves are crisp. Store at room temperature in an airtight container for up to a week.

PER SERVING

Calories: 99 – Fat: 7g – Sodium: 413mg – Fiber: 4g

Carbohydrates: 7g – Sugar: 2g – Protein: 3g

HOMEMADE TRAIL MIX
SERVES 5

This trail mix has less sugar than conventional trail mixes. For a different flavor, vary the nuts, seeds, or dried fruits. Perfect for mid-class snacking or a post-workout energy boost!

INGREDIENTS

1 cup plain granola

$\frac{1}{4}$ cup raw unsalted peanuts

$\frac{1}{4}$ cup semisweet chocolate chips

$\frac{1}{4}$ cup dehydrated banana chips

2 tablespoons whole hazelnuts

In a medium bowl, combine all the ingredients. Pack in a resealable plastic bag or container for easy carrying. If not using immediately, store in an airtight container.

PER SERVING ($\frac{1}{3}$ CUP)

Calories: 242 – Fat: 14g – Sodium: 8mg – Fiber: 4g

Carbohydrates: 25g – Sugar: 13g – Protein: 7g

ROASTED PARSNIP CHIPS
SERVES 6

This is a simple recipe that yields a crisp, irresistible snack. Parsnips have a subtly sweet taste but won't have as much of an effect on your blood sugar as the white potatoes used in regular chips. They make a sturdy chip for dipping.

INGREDIENTS

6 large parsnips, peeled and cut diagonally into thin slices

3 tablespoons olive oil

$\frac{1}{8}$ teaspoon ground nutmeg

1 teaspoon ground cinnamon

1. Preheat oven to 400°F. Spray a large baking sheet with cooking spray.

2. In a large bowl, combine parsnips, olive oil, and spices and stir to coat.

3. Arrange parsnips on prepared baking sheet in a single layer and cook for 30 minutes. Remove from oven and turn on broiler. Broil chips for 5 minutes. Serve warm or at room temperature.

PER SERVING

Calories: 160 — Fat: 7g — Sodium: 13mg — Fiber: 7g

Carbohydrates: 24g — Sugar: 6g — Protein: 2g

NO-BAKE TEX-MEX NACHOS
SERVES 4

You'll be glad you skipped the campus meal plan after trying these No-Bake Tex-Mex Nachos. Tex-Mex is an abbreviation of Texan-Mexican, a term used to describe a regional American cuisine that blends foods available in the United States with the culinary creations of Mexico. Garnish with fresh pico de gallo and chopped jalapeño for a more authentic taste.

INGREDIENTS

$4\frac{1}{2}$ ounces tortilla chips

$1\frac{1}{2}$ cups canned chili-style red kidney beans, drained and rinsed

2 teaspoons vegetable oil

2 tablespoons low-fat plain Greek yogurt

$\frac{1}{2}$ cup grated Cheddar cheese

1. Lay the tortilla chips on a large baking sheet.

2. In a small bowl, mash the beans by hand, or purée in a food processor.

3. In a small skillet over medium heat, warm the oil. Add the mashed kidney beans and heat through, stirring. Stir in yogurt.

4. Carefully spoon the kidney bean mixture onto the tortilla chips. Sprinkle with the grated cheese and serve.

PER SERVING

Calories: 312 — Fat: 13g — Sodium: 314mg — Fiber: 6g

Carbohydrates: 34g — Sugar: 1g — Protein: 11g

CHOCOLATE NUT BARS
SERVES 16

Instead of picking up a candy bar at the convenience store after class, try these Chocolate Nut Bars. Stash a few in your backpack for those moments when you're craving a little something sweet. Make sure you use good-quality chocolate with as few ingredients as possible.

INGREDIENTS

1 cup hazelnuts

1 cup walnuts

1½ cups pecans

1 pound dark chocolate, cut into small pieces

1. Preheat oven to 350°F. Place hazelnuts, walnuts, and pecans on a large baking sheet. Bake for 10–15 minutes or just until nuts are fragrant and start to brown. Remove from oven and cool completely.

2. Coarsely chop nuts and place on a large baking sheet lined with parchment paper.

3. Reserve ⅓ cup chocolate; place remaining chocolate in a small, heavy saucepan over low heat. Melt, stirring occasionally, until the mixture is smooth. Remove from heat and stir in reserved chocolate until melted; this tempers the chocolate so it will stay solid at room temperature.

4. Pour chocolate over nuts to coat. Let stand until set, then break into bars. Store in airtight container at room temperature for up to a week.

PER SERVING
Calories: 334 – Fat: 31g – Sodium: 7mg – Fiber: 6g
Carbohydrates: 12g – Sugar: 3g – Protein: 6g

ITALIAN PESTO POPCORN
MAKES 15 CUPS

This Italian Pesto Popcorn makes a great snack to bring to class—or to just enjoy while sitting at home watching a movie with your roommates. If pesto isn't your favorite, use any other spices you like!

INGREDIENTS

$\frac{1}{3}$ cup unsalted butter

1 teaspoon dried basil

$\frac{1}{4}$ teaspoon garlic salt

2 teaspoons grated Parmesan cheese

15 cups popped popcorn

1. In a small saucepan, melt the butter over low heat. Stir in the basil, garlic salt, and cheese.

2. Spread the popcorn out on a large tray. Slowly pour the melted butter mixture over the popcorn, stirring to make sure it is mixed thoroughly.

PER SERVING (1 CUP)
Calories: 68 – Fat: 4g – Sodium: 38mg – Fiber: 1g
Carbohydrates: 6g – Sugar: 0g – Protein: 1g

ROASTED PISTACHIOS
SERVES 16

Raw shelled pistachios are available at Trader Joe's and health food stores. Roasting your own lets you avoid salt on the nuts, which makes them a snack that perfectly matches your healthy palate. But take it easy on the serving size for these delicious nibbles: Though pistachios are super good for you, they're also super high in fat.

INGREDIENTS

1 pound raw pistachios

2 tablespoons olive oil

1. Add nuts and olive oil to a 2-quart slow cooker. Stir to combine. Cover and cook on low for 1 hour.

2. Stir the mixture again. Cover and cook for 2 more hours, stirring the mixture again after 1 hour. Cool and store in an airtight container in the refrigerator for up to several months.

PER SERVING

Calories: 174 – Fat: 14g – Sodium: 0mg – Fiber: 3g
Carbohydrates: 8g – Sugar: 2g – Protein: 6g

GRAHAM CRACKERS
MAKES 30 CRACKERS

There are many gluten-free flour substitutes on the market. Coconut and hazelnut flours are naturally sweet, and this gluten-free vegan cracker has a mild, nutty taste. Enjoy with s'mores at a bonfire with friends!

INGREDIENTS

1 cup hazelnut flour

$\frac{3}{4}$ cup coconut flour

$\frac{1}{4}$ cup tapioca starch

$\frac{1}{4}$ teaspoon baking soda

$\frac{1}{2}$ teaspoon cream of tartar

2 teaspoons ground cinnamon

$\frac{1}{4}$ teaspoon salt

$\frac{1}{3}$ cup maple syrup

3 tablespoons coconut oil

$\frac{1}{4}$ cup canned full-fat coconut milk

1 tablespoon water

2 teaspoons vanilla extract

1. Preheat oven to 350°F. In a large bowl, combine hazelnut flour, coconut flour, tapioca starch, baking soda, cream of tartar, cinnamon, and salt, and mix until one color.

2. In a small saucepan over medium heat, combine maple syrup, coconut oil, coconut milk, and water and heat until oil melts.

3. Add the coconut milk mixture to the dry ingredients along with vanilla and mix until dough forms. You may need to add a touch more of either of the flours or more water for the right consistency (it should be dough-like). Wrap in plastic wrap and refrigerate for 1 hour.

4. Line a large baking sheet with parchment paper. Roll dough into 2" balls and place on lined baking sheet about 3" apart. Top with another sheet of parchment paper and flatten balls using a rolling pin to $\frac{1}{8}$" thickness. Carefully peel off the top piece of paper. Prick the dough with a fork.

5. Bake for 12–15 minutes or until crackers are set and golden brown. Cool on wire racks. Store in an airtight container at room temperature for up to a week.

PER SERVING (1 CRACKER)
Calories: 62 — Fat: 4g — Sodium: 32mg — Fiber: 2g
Carbohydrates: 6g — Sugar: 3g — Protein: 1g

VEGGIE-PACKED POTATO SKINS
SERVES 12

Dining hall versions of potato skins often have unhealthy ingredients and are topped with even more of the same; you can enjoy a healthier version of the same food that packs flavor, texture, and tons of nutrition…without the guilt and bloat of the alternative.

INGREDIENTS

6 large Idaho potatoes, baked

1 tablespoon olive oil

1 cup chopped red onion

1 cup chopped zucchini

1 cup sliced button mushrooms

2 tablespoons water

1 teaspoon salt, divided

1 teaspoon ground black pepper, divided

1 teaspoon garlic powder, divided

1 teaspoon ground cumin, divided

1 cup plain soy yogurt

3 medium Roma tomatoes, chopped

1. Allow potatoes to cool after baking, cut in half lengthwise, and scoop out the inside of the potatoes leaving $1/8$"–$1/4$" of flesh. Save 1 cup of scooped potatoes for the stuffing mixture.

2. In a large skillet over medium heat, heat olive oil until runny and smooth. Sauté onion about 2 minutes or until slightly tender. Add zucchini, mushrooms, and water to the onions. Sprinkle with $1/2$ teaspoon each of the salt, pepper, garlic powder, and cumin; sauté 5–6 minutes or until fork-tender.

3. Move the sautéed vegetables to the mixing bowl and combine thoroughly with the potatoes. Add the yogurt and remaining salt, pepper, garlic powder, and cumin; mix together until chunky and well combined.

4. Spoon the mixture into the potato skins and pack by pressing firmly. Garnish with chopped tomatoes.

PER SERVING
Calories: 151 – Fat: 1g – Sodium: 211mg – Fiber: 3g
Carbohydrates: 31g – Sugar: 4g – Protein: 4g

GINGER VEGETABLE SPRING ROLLS

SERVES 12

You may be surprised to see that there are now vegan spring roll wrappers available, but it's true! Especially in college towns, grocery stores and health food stores are responding to the needs of those looking to adopt a more plant-based diet; you'll be amazed by the variety of available options. And if you don't see something you're looking for in the store, just ask; the manager might want to stock the product if enough people show an interest.

INGREDIENTS

I cup shredded red cabbage

$\frac{1}{2}$ cup shredded carrot

$\frac{1}{2}$ cup chopped green onion

$\frac{1}{2}$ cup chopped celery

$\frac{1}{2}$ cup diced extra-firm tofu

I tablespoon grated fresh ginger

2 teaspoons minced fresh garlic

2 tablespoons sesame oil

2 tablespoons soy sauce

12 ($8\frac{1}{2}$") vegan spring roll wrappers

2 tablespoons water

I tablespoon vegetable oil

1. Preheat oven to 425°F and prepare an oven grate with olive oil spray.

2. In a large bowl, combine cabbage, carrots, onion, celery, tofu, ginger, and garlic. Add sesame oil and soy sauce to the mixture and blend well until ingredients are combined thoroughly and wet.

3. In the center of each spring roll wrapper, place 2 tablespoons of the vegetable mixture. Fold wrappers as when wrapping enchiladas: Wet the edges of the wrapper, fold in the right and left sides to cover edges of mixture, and roll to enclose completely.

4. Lay the spring rolls on the prepared grate; use fingers or a pastry brush to lightly coat the spring rolls with the vegetable oil.

5. Bake 15 minutes, turn, and continue baking an additional 5–10 minutes or until spring rolls are brown and crispy.

PER SERVING

Calories: 56 — Fat: 2g — Sodium: 209mg — Fiber: 0g

Carbohydrates: 9g — Sugar: 1g — Protein: 1g

SPICY WHITE BEAN CITRUS DIP
SERVES 12

Tangy, spicy, unique, and easy to throw together, this stupendous dip is perfect for the big game pre-party! Serve with Baked Tortilla Chips (see recipe in Chapter 8), Roasted Parsnip Chips (see recipe in this chapter), or raw vegetables.

INGREDIENTS

2 (15-ounce) cans white navy beans, drained and rinsed

$\frac{1}{4}$ cup sour cream

1 tablespoon orange juice

1 teaspoon hot pepper sauce

1 teaspoon lime juice

Grated zest of 1 medium orange

$\frac{1}{2}$ teaspoon salt

$\frac{1}{2}$ cup diced white onion

1 tablespoon chopped fresh cilantro

1. Purée beans, sour cream, orange juice, hot pepper sauce, lime juice, orange zest, and salt in a food processor or blender until smooth.

2. Add onions and cilantro; mix with a rubber spatula until combined.

PER SERVING
Calories: 100 – Fat: 1g – Sodium: 314mg – Fiber: 4g
Carbohydrates: 17g – Sugar: 1g – Protein: 6g

Smoky and Spicy
For a smokier taste, replace the hot pepper sauce with puréed chipotle pepper. Chipotle is a smoked jalapeño pepper. They are sold in small 6-ounce cans, and are very useful for imparting a smoky flavor and medium heat to dishes. Purée them with the sauce in which they're packed, using a blender or food processor.

ROASTED CASHEW AND SPICY BASIL PESTO

SERVES 3

You'll need fresh basil (in bunches in the produce aisle) for making pesto. This recipe calls for Thai basil, but for a more traditional Italian pesto, you can use regular Italian basil. If you do use Italian instead of Thai basil, cut back on the garlic a bit, and use pine nuts or walnuts instead of roasted cashews. Although pesto is commonly used as a pasta sauce, you can also serve it with crackers and cut vegetables; it makes a tasty dip!

INGREDIENTS

4 medium cloves garlic, peeled

1 cup Thai basil, packed

$\frac{2}{3}$ cup roasted cashews

$\frac{1}{2}$ cup nutritional yeast

$\frac{1}{4}$ teaspoon salt

$\frac{1}{2}$ teaspoon ground black pepper

$\frac{1}{3}$ cup olive oil

Place all ingredients except the olive oil in blender or food processor and blend until smooth. Slowly incorporate olive oil until desired consistency is reached.

PER SERVING

Calories: 434 – Fat: 38g – Sodium: 216mg – Fiber: 3g

Carbohydrates: 15g – Sugar: 2g – Protein: 11g

CHEWY GRANOLA BARS
MAKES 16 BARS

Most commercial granola bars are loaded with processed sugar, preservatives, and artificial ingredients. Make your own healthy granola bars for a satisfying snack after classes. You can vary the nuts and dried fruits in these bars as you like.

INGREDIENTS

8 tablespoons coconut oil

$\frac{1}{4}$ cup honey

2 cups rolled oats

2 tablespoons toasted wheat germ

$\frac{3}{4}$ teaspoon ground cinnamon

I tablespoon sesame seeds

2 large eggs

$\frac{1}{2}$ cup raisins

$\frac{1}{2}$ cup chopped peanuts

1. Preheat oven to 300°F.

2. In a small saucepan over low heat, melt coconut oil with honey, stirring continuously.

3. In a large bowl, combine oats, wheat germ, cinnamon, and sesame seeds. Add melted oil and honey to the dry ingredients, and stir to mix.

4. In a small bowl, lightly beat the eggs and then add them to the oat mixture, stirring to combine. Stir in the raisins and peanuts.

5. Line a 9" × 9" pan with parchment paper or tin foil. Spread the oat mixture in the lined pan, using a rubber spatula to press it down and distribute it evenly.

6. Bake 15 minutes or until golden brown. Let cool and cut into sixteen bars.

PER SERVING (1 BAR)
Calories: 187 – Fat: 10g – Sodium: 10mg – Fiber: 2g
Carbohydrates: 20g – Sugar: 10g – Protein: 4g

TOMATO AND DILL–STUFFED GRAPE LEAVES (DOLMAS)
MAKES 24 DOLMAS

Enjoy with tabbouleh for a classic Middle Eastern dish. When you're in a hurry between classes, mix together some leftover rice with vegan pesto for this recipe's filling. Wrap, simmer just a few minutes, and eat!

INGREDIENTS

3 medium scallions, chopped

1 medium tomato, diced small

1/4 cup olive oil, divided

1 cup uncooked brown rice

1/2 cup water

1/2 teaspoon salt

1 tablespoon chopped fresh dill

1 teaspoon dried parsley

1 tablespoon chopped fresh mint

24 grape leaves

Water for boiling

2 tablespoons lemon juice

1. In a medium skillet, heat scallions and tomato in 2 tablespoons olive oil for 2 minutes, then add rice, water, salt, dill, parsley, and mint. Cover and cook for 5 minutes. Remove from heat and cool.

2. Place about 2 teaspoons of the rice filling in the center of a grape leaf near the stem. Fold the bottom of the leaf over the filling, then fold in the sides, and roll. Continue with each grape leaf.

3. Line the bottom of a large deep skillet with extra or torn grape leaves to prevent burning. Add wrapped and filled leaves, then add enough water to just cover the dolmas. Add remaining 2 tablespoons olive oil and bring to a slow simmer over medium heat.

4. Cook for 20 minutes. Drizzle with lemon juice just before serving.

PER SERVING (1 DOLMA)
Calories: 52 – Fat: 2g – Sodium: 49mg – Fiber: 1g
Carbohydrates: 7g – Sugar: 0g – Protein: 1g

FRIED ZUCCHINI STICKS
SERVES 4

Skip the dining hall French fries, and try these delicious Fried Zucchini Sticks instead. In this recipe you fry the zucchini, but for a lighter version you can just sauté them in a bit of oil. This makes a great appetizer or snack.

INGREDIENTS

$3/4$ cup all-purpose flour

$1/2$ teaspoon garlic powder

$3/4$ teaspoon Italian seasoning

$1/4$ teaspoon salt

4 medium zucchini, cut into strips

$1/3$ cup vegetable oil

1. In a large bowl or pan, combine flour, garlic powder, Italian seasoning, and salt.

2. Lightly toss the zucchini strips with the flour mixture, coating well.

3. Heat oil over medium heat in a large skillet or frying pan. When oil is hot, gently add zucchini strips to pan. Fry until lightly golden brown on all sides.

PER SERVING
Calories: 244 – Fat: 18g – Sodium: 12mg – Fiber: 2g
Carbohydrates: 16g – Sugar: 5g – Protein: 4g

VEGAN TZATZIKI
MAKES 3½ CUPS

This recipe uses vegan soy yogurt to give a plant-based update to tzatziki, a classic Greek dip that's best served very cold. A nondairy sour cream may be used instead of the soy yogurt, if you prefer.

INGREDIENTS

1½ cups plain soy yogurt

1 tablespoon olive oil

1 tablespoon lemon juice

4 medium cloves garlic, peeled and minced

2 medium cucumbers, chopped fine

1 tablespoon chopped fresh mint

1. In a medium bowl, whisk together yogurt with olive oil and lemon juice until well combined.

2. Combine with remaining ingredients.

3. Chill for at least 1 hour before serving to allow flavors to mingle. Serve cold.

PER SERVING (¼ CUP)
Calories: 32 – Fat: 1g – Sodium: 4mg – Fiber: 0g
Carbohydrates: 4g – Sugar: 2g – Protein: 1g

What Is Tzatziki?
Tzatziki is a Greek appetizer that is also used as a sauce for Greek dishes such as souvlaki and gyros. It is made of strained yogurt (usually sheep's milk or goat's milk varieties) with cucumbers, garlic, salt, olive oil, and pepper. Some variations also include lemon juice and parsley or mint.

AVOCADO AND SHIITAKE POT STICKERS

MAKES 12 POT STICKERS

Otherwise known as dumplings, pot stickers are traditionally served in Chinese restaurants with a little bowl of freshly grated ginger, and diners create a simple dipping sauce from the various condiments on the table. To try it, pour some rice vinegar and a touch of soy sauce over a bit of ginger and add hot chili oil to taste.

INGREDIENTS

1 large ripe avocado, peeled, pitted, and diced

$\frac{1}{2}$ cup diced shiitake mushrooms

$\frac{1}{2}$ block silken tofu, crumbled

1 medium clove garlic, peeled and minced

2 teaspoons balsamic vinegar

1 teaspoon soy sauce

12 (3") vegan dumpling wrappers

Water for steaming

1. In a small bowl, gently mash together all ingredients, except wrappers and water, just until mixed and crumbly.

2. Place about 1$\frac{1}{2}$ teaspoons of the filling in the middle of each wrapper. Fold in half and pinch closed, forming little pleats. You may want to dip your fingertips in water to help the dumplings stay sealed if needed.

3. To steam: Carefully place a layer of dumplings in a steamer, being sure the dumplings don't touch. Place steamer above boiling water and allow to cook, covered, for 3–4 minutes.

PER SERVING (1 POT STICKER)
Calories: 45 — Fat: 2g — Sodium: 60mg — Fiber: 1g
Carbohydrates: 5g — Sugar: 0g — Protein: 2g

CHILI CHEESE DIP
SERVES 12

Most major grocery stores sell canned vegetarian chili. One of the easiest to find is Hormel Vegetarian Chili with Beans. Or try the recipe for Vegan Chili in Chapter 5. Serve with Baked Tortilla Chips (see recipe in Chapter 8).

INGREDIENTS

1 (15-ounce) can vegetarian chili

¼ cup diced white onion

½ cup diced tomatoes

1 (8-ounce) package vegan cream cheese, cubed

1 cup shredded vegan Cheddar cheese

1 teaspoon garlic powder

1. Place all ingredients in a 4-quart slow cooker. (If you don't have a slow cooker, combine all ingredients in a large saucepan and simmer over medium-low heat for about 20 minutes, until cheeses melt.)

2. Stir gently; cover and heat on low for 1 hour. Serve warm.

PER SERVING
Calories: 115 – Fat: 8g – Sodium: 348mg – Fiber: 2g
Carbohydrates: 11g – Sugar: 1g – Protein: 2g

SIMPLE SCALLION PANCAKES
MAKES 6 LARGE PANCAKES

Whether you eat them as an accompaniment to a Chinese feast, or just as a snack or appetizer, these salty fried pancakes are a popular street food snack served up hot in East Asia. Plain soy sauce is the perfect dip.

INGREDIENTS

2 cups all-purpose flour

$1/2$ teaspoon salt

$2^1/_2$ teaspoons sesame oil, divided

$3/4$ cup hot water

6 medium scallions, chopped (green parts only)

$1/8$ cup vegetable oil

1. In a large bowl, combine flour and salt. Slowly add 2 teaspoons sesame oil and water, mixing just until a dough forms. You may need a little bit less than $3/4$ cup water.

2. Knead dough for a few minutes, then let sit for 30 minutes.

3. Divide dough into six (2") balls. Roll out each ball on a lightly floured surface. Brush with remaining sesame oil and cover with scallions. Roll up dough and twist to form a ball. Roll out again to $1/4$" thickness.

4. In a medium frying pan over medium-high heat, fry each pancake in hot oil 1–2 minutes on each side. Slice into squares or wedges and serve with soy sauce.

PER SERVING (1 PANCAKE)
Calories: 214 – Fat: 7g – Sodium: 196mg – Fiber: 2g
Carbohydrates: 33g – Sugar: 0g – Protein: 5g

MEXICAN LOADED FRENCH FRIES

SERVES 3

This cross between French fries and nachos might sound unhealthy, but these Mexican Loaded French Fries are made with clean ingredients, and the fries are baked, not fried. The perfect post-finals treat!

INGREDIENTS

2 large russet potatoes, peeled and sliced into thin, fry-sized wedges

2 tablespoons olive oil

1 large ripe avocado, halved and pitted

2 tablespoons lemon juice

$\frac{1}{2}$ teaspoon garlic powder

$\frac{1}{4}$ teaspoon salt

$\frac{1}{4}$ teaspoon ground black pepper

1 cup canned black beans, drained and rinsed

$\frac{3}{4}$ cup chopped cherry tomatoes

2 small green onions, finely chopped

2 tablespoons assorted microgreens

1. Preheat oven to 425°F. Line a 10" × 15" baking sheet with aluminum foil. Spread potatoes evenly onto baking sheet and drizzle with olive oil. Bake 10 minutes and then remove from oven. Turn potatoes and bake another 15 minutes. Potatoes should be crisp on the outside but soft inside.

2. While potatoes are baking, scoop out avocado and place it in a medium bowl. Add lemon juice, garlic powder, salt, and pepper, and mash with a fork.

3. When potatoes are ready, top with black beans, tomatoes, green onion, avocado mash, and microgreens. Serve immediately.

PER SERVING

Calories: 339 — Fat: 15g — Sodium: 386mg — Fiber: 11g

Carbohydrates: 43g — Sugar: 4g — Protein: 9g

TRAIL MIX CRUNCH
SERVES 8

If you sometimes miss store-bought potato chips and other crunchy snacks, this is the trail mix for you. It has a sweet and salty taste to satisfy your cravings, and it's vegan!

INGREDIENTS

$\frac{1}{2}$ cup cashews

$\frac{1}{2}$ cup almonds

$\frac{1}{2}$ cup macadamia nuts

$\frac{1}{2}$ cup pistachios

4 tablespoons maple syrup

1 teaspoon salt

$\frac{1}{2}$ teaspoon ground black pepper

$\frac{1}{4}$ teaspoon ground cumin

1 teaspoon curry powder

$\frac{1}{8}$ teaspoon ground cloves

1 teaspoon ground cinnamon

1. Preheat oven to 300°F.

2. Place cashews, almonds, macadamias, and pistachios on a large baking sheet and bake for 10–12 minutes, taking care they do not burn. Remove from oven and let cool approximately 5 minutes.

3. In a small bowl, mix maple syrup, salt, pepper, cumin, curry powder, cloves, and cinnamon.

4. In a large saucepan over medium heat, place nuts and half the honey mixture. When the mixture begins to melt, mix in remaining honey mixture.

5. Shake the pan and stir until nuts are coated, about 5 minutes.

6. Remove nuts from the pan and spread them out on a sheet of parchment paper. Use a spoon to separate nuts that stick together. Let dry for about 30 minutes. Trail mix will keep for about a week in an airtight container at room temperature.

PER SERVING
Calories: 238 – Fat: 17g – Sodium: 29mg – Fiber: 3g
Carbohydrates: 15g – Sugar: 8g – Protein: 6g

CHAPTER 4

SANDWICHES AND SALADS

Asian Lettuce Wrap Sandwich...........80

Ultimate Veggie Wrap........................82

Greek Salad Pita Pockets..................84

Heirloom Tomato Sandwich..............85

Easy Falafel Patties...........................86

Black and Green Veggie Burritos.....87

Avocado Bagel Sandwich..................89

Baked Tortilla Wraps........................90

TLT: Tempeh Lettuce
Tomato Sandwich...............................91

Hummus with Tahini
in a Pita Pocket.................................92

Portobello Pita with
Buckwheat and Beans.......................93

Healthy Veggie Cuban.......................94

Tomato, Mozzarella,
and Spinach Salad.............................96

Sesame and Soy
Coleslaw Salad..................................97

Tangerine and Mint Salad.................98

Cucumber Cilantro Salad...................99

Colorful Vegetable
and Pasta Salad...............................101

Carrot and Date Salad 102

Tomato and Bread Salad
(Panzanella).....................................103

Winter Greens Salad with Green Beans
and Blue Cheese Vinaigrette............104

Asian Cucumber Salad.....................105

Strawberry, Walnut, and Flaxseed
Salad..106

Caesar Salad 108

Grilled Vegetable Antipasto...........109

Mixed Baby Greens with
Balsamic Vinaigrette........................110

Garden Salad with
Avocado and Sprouts.......................111

ASIAN LETTUCE WRAP SANDWICH

SERVES 2

Green, orange, and red bell peppers all actually come from the same plant. The color difference just depends on how long the peppers are left on the plant to ripen before picking. Extra ripening time gives red bell peppers a sweeter flavor than green bell peppers, making them a popular salad ingredient.

INGREDIENTS

2 teaspoons rice vinegar

2 teaspoons soy sauce

1 teaspoon honey

1 teaspoon cornstarch

2 teaspoons water

6 ounces tempeh

3 tablespoons vegetable oil, divided

1 medium clove garlic, peeled and crushed

3 tablespoons chopped white onion

$\frac{1}{3}$ cup chopped red bell pepper

$\frac{1}{4}$ cup bean sprouts

3 drops sesame oil

1 romaine lettuce leaf, shredded

4 (6") whole-wheat tortilla wraps

1. In a small bowl, combine rice vinegar, soy sauce, and honey, and set aside.

2. In a separate small bowl, mix cornstarch and water; set aside. Chop tempeh into bite-sized pieces.

3. Add 2 tablespoons vegetable oil to a medium frying pan and heat on medium-high heat. When oil is hot, add garlic. Fry briefly, using a spatula to move the garlic through the oil. Add tempeh and stir-fry until cooked on all sides, stirring constantly, about 7 minutes. Remove from the pan and set aside.

4. Add remaining tablespoon vegetable oil to the pan. Add onion and stir-fry for about 1 minute. Add red pepper and stir-fry for another minute. Add bean sprouts.

ASIAN LETTUCE WRAP SANDWICH CONT.

5. Add the rice vinegar mixture to the pan, pouring it in the middle of the vegetables. Give the corn-starch and water mixture a quick stir. Turn the heat up to medium-high and add the cornstarch mixture. Cook, stirring constantly, until it boils and thickens. Add the tempeh and mix with the vege-tables and sauce. Sprinkle sesame oil over the top.

6. Place a few pieces of shredded lettuce on each wrap, spoon one-fourth of the tempeh and sauce mixture over the top of each, and roll up. If using pita pocket halves, place the shredded lettuce and one-fourth of the tempeh mixture inside each half. If using a tortilla wrap, roll it up.

PER SERVING

Calories: 641 — Fat: 35g — Sodium: 741mg — Fiber: 9g

Carbohydrates: 54g — Sugar: 7g — Protein: 25g

ULTIMATE VEGGIE WRAP
SERVES 1

Sometimes it's hard to get your daily vegetables in as a college student. This recipe makes it easy! If you don't have alfalfa sprouts in your refrigerator, substitute broccoli instead. Use what you have.

INGREDIENTS

1 (12") spinach tortilla

$\frac{1}{2}$ cup fresh spinach leaves

1 tablespoon diced tomatoes

1 tablespoon sliced button mushrooms

1 tablespoon roasted red pepper

1 tablespoon chopped green pepper

$\frac{1}{4}$ cup alfalfa sprouts

1 tablespoon shredded carrots

1 tablespoon crumbled feta cheese

1 tablespoon balsamic vinegar

Lay tortilla flat on a plate. Pile other ingredients on top of tortilla. Roll tortilla into a wrap.

PER SERVING
Calories: 251 — Fat: 5g — Sodium: 708mg — Fiber: 2g
Carbohydrates: 42g — Sugar: 6g — Protein: 11g

GREEK SALAD PITA POCKETS
SERVES 1

Feta is a brined sheep's milk cheese traditionally made in Greece. It is an aged cheese, commonly produced in blocks, and has a slightly grainy texture. Bring these Greek Salad Pita Pockets for lunch when you have a long day on campus.

INGREDIENTS

1 (6") whole-wheat pita pocket bread

$\frac{1}{2}$ medium tomato

2 romaine lettuce leaves

8 cucumber slices

$\frac{1}{4}$ cup crumbled feta cheese

6 whole olives, chopped

2 tablespoons olive oil

$\frac{1}{8}$ teaspoon salt

$\frac{1}{8}$ teaspoon ground black pepper

1. Cut pita pocket in half. Cut tomato into thin wedges. Shred romaine lettuce leaves.

2. In a medium bowl, toss lettuce and tomato with cucumber.

3. Add feta, olives, and olive oil, and toss again. Sprinkle with salt and pepper.

4. Fill each pita half with half of the salad, and serve.

PER SERVING

Calories: 589 – Fat: 39g – Sodium: 1,294mg – Fiber: 9g
Carbohydrates: 49g – Sugar: 7g – Protein: 14g

HEIRLOOM TOMATO SANDWICH
SERVES 1

Select a rustic round loaf, such as a sourdough, and cut thick slices from the center for a full-sized sandwich. You'll find fresh mozzarella in a specialty cheese shop or the imported cheeses section of a well-stocked supermarket. Ask someone majoring in horticulture—or a farmer at your local farmers' market—to explain what makes a tomato "heirloom." They taste great, and make a "meaty" sandwich without the meat!

INGREDIENTS

1 teaspoon olive oil

2 thick slices whole-wheat sourdough bread

1 teaspoon minced fresh garlic

2 teaspoons mayonnaise

3 fresh basil leaves

1 large heirloom tomato, thinly sliced

2 thin slices fresh mozzarella cheese

$\frac{1}{8}$ teaspoon salt

$\frac{1}{8}$ teaspoon ground black pepper

1. Drizzle olive oil on one slice of the bread.

2. Mix together garlic and mayonnaise and spread the mixture on the other slice of bread.

3. Cover this slice with basil leaves. Top the leaves with tomato and mozzarella slices, layering slices if necessary. Sprinkle slices with salt and pepper and close the sandwich.

PER SERVING
Calories: 474 – Fat: 25g – Sodium: 829mg – Fiber: 8g
Carbohydrates: 41g – Sugar: 6g – Protein: 19g

EASY FALAFEL PATTIES
SERVES 4

This oven-baked falafel is simple to make and much healthier than what you might get from a street vendor or in a restaurant. Stuff the falafel into a pita bread with some sliced tomatoes and lettuce and top it off with a bit of tahini, Vegan Tzatziki (see recipe in Chapter 3), or hummus for an authentic (albeit lower-fat) Middle Eastern sandwich. Incorporate smaller falafel balls into your salads.

INGREDIENTS

1 (15-ounce) can chickpeas, drained and rinsed

½ medium white onion, peeled and minced

1 tablespoon all-purpose flour

1 teaspoon ground cumin

¾ teaspoon garlic powder

¾ teaspoon salt

1 large egg

¼ cup chopped fresh parsley

2 tablespoons chopped fresh cilantro

1. Preheat oven to 375°F.

2. Place chickpeas in a large bowl and mash with a fork until coarsely mashed. Or pulse in a food processor until chopped.

3. Combine chickpeas with onion, flour, cumin, garlic powder, salt, and egg, mashing together to combine. Add parsley and cilantro.

4. Shape the mixture into 2" balls or 1"-thick patties, place on a large baking sheet, and bake in oven for 15 minutes or until crisp. (The falafel patties can also be fried in oil for about 5–6 minutes on each side.)

PER SERVING
Calories: 122 – Fat: 2g – Sodium: 591mg – Fiber: 5g
Carbohydrates: 18g – Sugar: 3g – Protein: 7g

BLACK AND GREEN VEGGIE BURRITOS

MAKES 4 BURRITOS

Your roommates won't believe you didn't buy these burritos at the campus taqueria. For a gluten-free or more protein-packed version, use a cooked grain other than rice in these burritos and shop for a gluten-free flatbread to wrap it up in. Quinoa in particular works well in burritos, as it is lighter than other grains.

INGREDIENTS

1 medium white onion, peeled and chopped

2 medium zucchini, cut into thin strips

1 medium green bell pepper, seeded and chopped

2 tablespoons olive oil

$\frac{1}{2}$ teaspoon dried oregano

$\frac{1}{2}$ teaspoon ground cumin

1 (15-ounce) can black beans, drained

1 (4-ounce) can green chilies, drained

1 cup cooked brown rice

4 (12") whole-wheat tortillas, warmed

1. In a large frying pan, heat onion, zucchini, and bell pepper in olive oil over medium-low heat until vegetables are soft, about 4–5 minutes.

2. Reduce heat to low and add oregano, cumin, black beans, and chilies, combining well. Cook, stirring, until well combined and heated through.

3. Place $\frac{1}{4}$ cup rice in the center of each flour tortilla and top with the bean mixture.

4. Fold the bottom of the tortilla up, then snugly wrap one side, then the other. Serve as is, or bake in a 350°F oven for 15 minutes for a crispy burrito.

PER SERVING (1 BURRITO)
Calories: 378 — Fat: 11g — Sodium: 511mg — Fiber: 15g
Carbohydrates: 57g — Sugar: 7g — Protein: 13g

AVOCADO BAGEL SANDWICH
SERVES 1

This sandwich packs a plant-based punch with some delicious add-ons to the old standby cream cheese. For the bagel, choose one of the many different varieties available—from whole wheat to honey oat—that are better for you than the standard plain. This sandwich is on an untoasted bagel, so be sure to use a fresh, chewy one. You can also slice the bagel in thirds horizontally, adding another slice of onion and avocado.

INGREDIENTS

2 ounces whipped cream cheese

1 whole-wheat bagel, sliced

1 slice tomato

1 slice red onion

$\frac{1}{2}$ medium ripe avocado, peeled, pitted, and sliced

$\frac{1}{4}$ cup alfalfa sprouts

1. Spread cream cheese on both halves of the bagel.

2. Layer tomato, onion, avocado, and alfalfa sprouts on the bottom half of the bagel.

3. Top with the other half of the bagel and cut the sandwich in half.

PER SERVING
Calories: 495 – Fat: 21g – Sodium: 655mg – Fiber: 9g
Carbohydrates: 61g – Sugar: 10g – Protein: 15g

BAKED TORTILLA WRAPS
SERVES 2

Many cuisines have a special type of flatbread, from Middle Eastern pita to Indian naan and Mexican tortillas. If you'd like, swap out the tortillas in this recipe with your favorite type of flatbread.

INGREDIENTS

4 ounces tempeh

1 teaspoon olive oil

3 tablespoons chopped red onion

1/4 small green bell pepper, seeded and finely chopped

1 tablespoon red wine vinegar

2 (6") whole-wheat tortilla wraps

2 tablespoons creamy peanut butter

Flatbread 101
Despite their flat shape (and their name), some flatbreads contain a leavener (an ingredient to make the dough or batter rise). Double-layered breads (such as pita) may use either sourdough or yeast as a leavener, while single-layered Italian focaccia is always made with yeast.

1. Preheat oven to 350°F. Spray a medium baking sheet with cooking spray.

2. Cut tempeh into thin strips. Heat olive oil in a frying pan over medium heat. Add onion and cook until tender. Add green pepper and cook for 1–2 minutes.

3. Push the vegetables off to the side of the pan and add tempeh in the middle, laying the strips out flat. Splash red wine vinegar over tempeh. Cook until tempeh is browned on both sides, turning over once. Mix vegetables in with tempeh and vinegar. Remove from heat and let cool briefly.

4. Lay one tortilla wrap flat on a plate and spread peanut butter on the inside. Add half the tempeh and vegetable mixture on the bottom of the wrap, making sure the filling isn't too close to the edges. Fold in the right and left sides of the wrap. Roll up and tuck in the edges. Repeat with the other tortilla wrap.

5. Place both wraps on the prepared baking sheet. Bake for 15 minutes or until heated through.

PER SERVING
Calories: 359 – Fat: 19g – Sodium: 218mg – Fiber: 5g
Carbohydrates: 30g – Sugar: 4g – Protein: 18g

TLT: TEMPEH LETTUCE TOMATO SANDWICH
MAKES 3 SANDWICHES

This vegan take on a BLT uses tempeh "bacon," which is what makes it a TLT. The tempeh, seared and crisped to perfection in a maple pepper marinade, and combined with the classic ingredients of lettuce and tomato, will be just what you need to refuel after a big test.

INGREDIENTS

TEMPEH "BACON"

8 ounces organic tempeh

2 tablespoons olive oil

2 tablespoons maple syrup

1/4 teaspoon paprika

1/4 teaspoon cayenne pepper

1/4 teaspoon ground black pepper

SANDWICH

6 slices sprouted-grain bread

1 1/2 tablespoons vegan mayonnaise (such as Vegenaise)

1 medium ripe avocado, peeled and sliced

1 medium tomato, thinly sliced

6 butter lettuce leaves

1. For Tempeh "Bacon": Cut tempeh into three thin strips widthwise, then cut those strips in half lengthwise. Cut them in half once more, this time crosswise. You should have twelve baconlike strips that are about 1" wide and 3" long.

2. In a medium bowl, combine olive oil, maple syrup, paprika, cayenne pepper, and black pepper. Spread half the mixture onto one side of all the tempeh strips.

3. Heat a large frying pan on medium heat. Add tempeh (sauce-side down) and cook 5 minutes until golden and beginning to char. Coat the top with the remaining sauce and flip the tempeh; cook another 5 minutes.

4. For Sandwich: Toast bread. Spread mayonnaise on three slices of bread. Add tempeh, and top with avocado, tomato, and lettuce. Top with remaining slices of bread and serve immediately.

PER SERVING (1 SANDWICH)
Calories: 525 — Fat: 27g — Sodium: 190mg — Fiber: 9g
Carbohydrates: 48g — Sugar: 11g — Protein: 22g

HUMMUS WITH TAHINI IN A PITA POCKET

SERVES 4

These beautiful, healthful sandwiches are colorful, attractive, and quick to make. Serve with pepperoncini or other spicy pickles. Tahini is a paste made from ground sesame seeds and is carried by most larger supermarkets; look for it near the nut butters or in the ethnic foods aisle.

INGREDIENTS

- 1 (15.5-ounce) can chickpeas, drained and rinsed

- 2 tablespoons tahini

- 1 tablespoon ground cumin

- 2 tablespoons fresh lemon juice, divided

- $1/3$ cup plus 1 tablespoon olive oil, divided

- $1/8$ teaspoon coarse (kosher) salt

- $1/8$ teaspoon ground black pepper

- 4 (7") whole-wheat pita pocket breads

- 4 tablespoons alfalfa sprouts

- 12 ripe cherry tomatoes, washed and halved

1. Purée chickpeas, tahini, cumin, and half the lemon juice at high speed in a food processor or blender. While machine is running, gradually add $1/3$ cup olive oil, salt, pepper, and remaining lemon juice.

2. Make an opening at the top of each pita and slather each generously with hummus. Into each pocket, stuff a tuft of alfalfa sprouts the size of a golf ball and six cherry tomato halves. Drizzle remaining olive oil over contents of all sandwiches.

PER SERVING

Calories: 505 – Fat: 27g – Sodium: 478mg – Fiber: 10g
Carbohydrates: 55g – Sugar: 5g – Protein: 13g

The Great Tahini

That hard-to-define, slightly smoky, slightly nutty dimension to many Middle Eastern foods is a fine-ground sesame seed paste called tahini. It's excellent in dressings, and combines beautifully with anything containing chickpeas for both wonderful flavors and complete proteins.

PORTOBELLO PITA WITH BUCKWHEAT AND BEANS

SERVES 4

The college lifestyle is so busy; it can be hard to make time for healthy meals. This quick and easy lunch is perfect for a college student on the go. The buckwheat has an earthy and pilaf-like texture that makes this sandwich a main-course dish. You can buy the buckwheat groats online if you can't find it in the rice or ethnic food aisles in the grocery store.

INGREDIENTS

4 medium portobello mushrooms, stems removed

$1/8$ teaspoon coarse (kosher) salt

$1/8$ teaspoon ground black pepper

1 tablespoon olive oil

4 (8") whole-wheat pita pocket breads

2 tablespoons soy mayonnaise

1 cup buckwheat groats, cooked according to directions on package

$1/4$ pound green beans, cooked

1. Brush portobello caps clean (do not wash under water); season with salt and pepper. Heat oil in a large skillet over medium heat until very hot but not quite smoking. Cook mushrooms top-side down over high heat until cooked through, about 4 minutes. Small pools of juice should appear where the stem was removed.

2. Cut an opening in a pita; slather the inside with soy mayonnaise. Spoon in a layer of cooked buckwheat groats and add a quarter of the green beans. Stuff in one mushroom cap. Repeat with remaining pitas.

PER SERVING

Calories: 403 — Fat: 7g — Sodium: 451mg — Fiber: 12g
Carbohydrates: 80g — Sugar: 4g — Protein: 15g

Ungrainy Grains

Sometimes things aren't what they seem. Most people think of couscous as a grain, but it isn't; it's pasta. Some consider buckwheat a grain; it isn't. It's the seed of a fruit completely unrelated to any kind of wheat. FYI: Wild rice isn't rice at all, but the seed of a native American grass.

HEALTHY VEGGIE CUBAN
SERVES 1

The Cuban sandwich was originally created by Cuban workers, either in Cuba or in the Cuban immigrant communities of Florida. This version of the classic sandwich uses vegetables in place of meat. Made this way, it's a lot better for you, but still as delicious as the original.

INGREDIENTS

1/2 medium portobello mushroom, sliced

1/4 medium zucchini, sliced lengthwise

1/4 medium yellow squash, sliced lengthwise

1/4 medium red bell pepper, seeded and sliced

1/8 teaspoon salt

1/8 teaspoon ground black pepper

1 (4") portion whole-wheat Cuban (or French or Italian) bread

1 tablespoon Roasted Red Pepper Hummus (see recipe in Chapter 8)

1 teaspoon yellow mustard

1 slice fat-free Swiss cheese

1 slice sour pickle

1. Preheat oven to 400°F. Coat a medium nonstick baking pan with cooking spray and add mushroom, zucchini, squash, and red pepper to it. Season with salt and pepper.

2. Bake vegetables for 8 minutes, flip vegetables, then cook for about 6–8 minutes or until brown.

3. Remove vegetables from pan and refrigerate for at least 1 hour.

4. Slice bread in half. Spread Roasted Red Pepper Hummus on the top half and mustard on the bottom half.

5. Top bottom slice of bread with vegetables, cheese, and pickle, then cover with top slice.

6. Coat nonstick frying pan with cooking spray. Place sandwich in pan and cook each side for 3 minutes over medium heat.

PER SERVING
Calories: 251 – Fat: 4g – Sodium: 988mg – Fiber: 6g
Carbohydrates: 39g – Sugar: 6g – Protein: 17g

TOMATO, MOZZARELLA, AND SPINACH SALAD
SERVES 2

The deli slices at the dining hall are probably heavily processed and not that nutritious. Fresh mozzarella is a natural alternative that's very versatile, minimally processed, and tastes great.

INGREDIENTS

2 cups fresh baby spinach leaves

1 cup chopped tomatoes

$\frac{1}{2}$ cup chopped fresh mozzarella cheese

2 tablespoons olive oil

2 teaspoons dried basil

1. Set out two salad bowls and split the spinach evenly between the two.

2. Top each salad with half the tomatoes and half the mozzarella.

3. Drizzle olive oil over the top of both salads and sprinkle with the dried basil.

PER SERVING
Calories: 143 – Fat: 24g – Sodium: 252mg – Fiber: 2g
Carbohydrates: 5g – Sugar: 3g – Protein: 12g

SESAME AND SOY COLESLAW SALAD
SERVES 4

Good news: You don't need mayonnaise to make a crispy, delicious coleslaw! This version is a refreshing alternative to traditional coleslaw. The sesame seeds give it a nice, nutty flavor. And it's *all* plant-based.

INGREDIENTS

1 medium head Napa cabbage, shredded

1 large carrot, peeled and grated

2 medium green onions, chopped

1 medium red bell pepper, seeded and sliced thin

2 tablespoons olive oil

2 tablespoons apple cider vinegar

2 teaspoons soy sauce

$\frac{1}{2}$ teaspoon sesame oil

2 tablespoons maple syrup

2 tablespoons sesame seeds

1. Toss together cabbage, carrot, green onions, and bell pepper in a large bowl.

2. In a separate small bowl, whisk together olive oil, vinegar, soy sauce, sesame oil, and maple syrup until well combined.

3. Drizzle dressing over cabbage and vegetable mix, add sesame seeds, and toss well to combine.

PER SERVING
Calories: 194 — Fat: 9g — Sodium: 202mg — Fiber: 8g
Carbohydrates: 25g — Sugar: 16g — Protein: 5g

TANGERINE AND MINT SALAD
SERVES 2

Fennel and mint are a wonderful combination, but the sweet tangerines will carry the salad if you can't find fennel. A small drizzle of gourmet oil, if you have some, would kick up the flavor even more. Try walnut or avocado oil.

INGREDIENTS

1 medium head green lettuce, chopped

2 tablespoons chopped fresh mint

2 medium tangerines, peeled and sectioned

1/3 cup chopped walnuts

1 medium bulb fennel, sliced thin

2 tablespoons olive oil

1/8 teaspoon salt

1/8 teaspoon ground black pepper

Gently toss together lettuce, mint, tangerines, walnuts, and sliced fennel. Drizzle with olive oil, salt, and pepper.

PER SERVING

Calories: 367 – Fat: 26g – Sodium: 233mg – Fiber: 10g
Carbohydrates: 31g – Sugar: 20g – Protein: 8g

CUCUMBER CILANTRO SALAD
SERVES 3

Cucumbers are heralded for their high water content. They also contain lignans, which scientists believe might have a role in preventing disease. In this recipe, cooling cucumbers and creamy yogurt are coupled with a dash of cayenne pepper for a salad that keeps you guessing; it's refreshing in any season.

INGREDIENTS

4 medium cucumbers, diced

2 medium tomatoes, chopped

$\frac{1}{2}$ medium red onion, peeled and diced

1 cup plain soy yogurt

1 tablespoon lemon juice

2 tablespoons chopped fresh cilantro

$\frac{1}{8}$ teaspoon salt

$\frac{1}{8}$ teaspoon ground black pepper

$\frac{1}{4}$ teaspoon cayenne pepper

Toss together all ingredients, stirring well to combine. Chill for at least 2 hours before serving, to allow flavors to blend. Toss again just before serving.

PER SERVING
Calories: 136 — Fat: 1g — Sodium: 119mg — Fiber: 4g
Carbohydrates: 28g — Sugar: 14g — Protein: 6g

COLORFUL VEGETABLE AND PASTA SALAD
SERVES 2

You're probably familiar with green peppers as a pizza topping, but peppers come in other colors and aren't just for pizza. A medium yellow or orange pepper has almost 300 percent of the daily recommended value of vitamin C, and can lend health benefits and a delightfully fruity taste to any dish. Serve as an appetizer at your next party, or make a large batch to have on hand for the week.

INGREDIENTS

1 large yellow pepper, seeded and sliced

1 large red pepper, seeded and sliced

1 cup sliced yellow onion

1 cup sliced zucchini

1 tablespoon olive oil

1 teaspoon salt

2 cups cooked whole-wheat rigatoni

2 tablespoons balsamic vinegar

1. In a large skillet over medium heat, sauté the sliced vegetables with the olive oil and salt until tender, about 5 minutes.

2. Remove the vegetables from the heat and allow to cool.

3. In a large bowl, combine the sautéed vegetables, cooked pasta, and balsamic until thoroughly combined.

PER SERVING
Calories: 317 — Fat: 9g — Sodium: 1,182mg — Fiber: 9g
Carbohydrates: 53g — Sugar: 12g — Protein: 10g

CARROT AND DATE SALAD
SERVES 4

This recipe is an update to the carrot and raisin salad—often made with pineapple and drowning in mayonnaise—you may have encountered in cafeteria salad bars. The sweetness of the dates and the clementines is tempered by the tahini (sesame paste). Look for dates near the dried fruits and nuts in the grocery store; tahini should be near the nut butters or in the ethnic foods aisle.

INGREDIENTS

⅓ cup tahini

1 tablespoon olive oil

2 tablespoons maple syrup

3 tablespoons lemon juice

¼ teaspoon salt

4 large carrots, peeled and grated

½ cup chopped dates

3 medium clementines, peeled and sectioned

⅓ cup unsweetened coconut flakes

1. In a small bowl, whisk together tahini, olive oil, maple syrup, lemon juice, and salt.

2. Place carrots in a large bowl, and toss well with the tahini mixture. Add dates, clementines, and coconut flakes and combine well.

3. Allow to sit for at least 1 hour before serving to soften carrots and dates. Toss again before serving.

PER SERVING
Calories: 328 – Fat: 17g – Sodium: 212mg – Fiber: 7g
Carbohydrates: 42g – Sugar: 27g – Protein: 6g

TOMATO AND BREAD SALAD (PANZANELLA)

SERVES 4

This panzanella, a favorite side dish served with sliced cheeses in Italy, might make you consider a study-abroad trip. Use both yellow and red tomatoes (the ripest you can find) to add a festive touch to your plate.

INGREDIENTS

2 cups ($\frac{1}{2}$"-cubed) day-old whole-wheat bread

2 cups diced red tomatoes, any variety

$\frac{1}{4}$ cup finely chopped red onion

$\frac{1}{2}$ teaspoon salt

$1\frac{1}{2}$ tablespoons olive oil

2 teaspoons fresh lemon juice

$\frac{1}{4}$ cup roughly chopped fresh basil

$\frac{1}{8}$ teaspoon ground black pepper

1. Preheat oven to 325°F. Bake bread cubes for 20 minutes.

2. In a medium bowl, combine tomatoes and onion with salt, olive oil, and lemon juice.

3. Toss gently with dried bread cubes and basil.

4. Season with black pepper.

PER SERVING
Calories: 178 – Fat: 6g – Sodium: 500mg – Fiber: 4g
Carbohydrates: 24g – Sugar: 5g – Protein: 7g

WINTER GREENS SALAD WITH GREEN BEANS AND BLUE CHEESE VINAIGRETTE
SERVES 4

Although known as winter greens, Belgium endive and watercress can be found year-round in larger markets with decent produce sections. The nutrition profile of these salad fixings puts iceberg lettuce to shame. Add chickpeas to make this dish a more complete meal.

INGREDIENTS

$\frac{1}{2}$ pound green beans

5 ounces watercress, torn into bite-sized pieces

2 medium heads Belgium endive, cored and chopped

1 small red onion, peeled and sliced

$\frac{1}{3}$ cup balsamic vinegar

$\frac{1}{3}$ cup vegetable oil

$\frac{1}{3}$ cup olive oil

1 tablespoon chopped fresh chives

$\frac{1}{4}$ pound blue cheese

$\frac{1}{8}$ teaspoon coarse (kosher) salt

$\frac{1}{8}$ teaspoon ground black pepper

1. In 3 quarts of rapidly boiling salted water, cook green beans in two separate batches until just tender, about 5 minutes, then plunge them into salted ice water to stop the cooking process. Drain green beans and place in a large bowl.

2. Add watercress, endive, and onion to the bowl with the green beans.

3. In a small bowl, whisk together vinegar, vegetable oil, olive oil, and chives. Roughly break the blue cheese into the dressing; stir with a spoon, leaving some large chunks. Season with salt and pepper.

4. Dress salad with $\frac{1}{3}$ cup of dressing. Remaining dressing will keep, refrigerated, for two weeks.

5. Arrange salad onto four plates, with onion rings and green beans displayed prominently on top.

PER SERVING
Calories: 516 − Fat: 44g − Sodium: 585mg − Fiber: 10g
Carbohydrates: 20g − Sugar: 6g − Protein: 11g

ASIAN CUCUMBER SALAD

SERVES 4

This refreshing, crisp salad pairs well with hearty fare such as grilled tempeh. Or add some to a sandwich for an extra crunch. With just a few ingredients, it's perfect for a day when your schedule is packed and there's not much time for cooking.

INGREDIENTS

¼ cup rice wine vinegar

1 teaspoon sugar

1 teaspoon chopped jalapeño pepper

1 large cucumber, peeled

2 drops sesame oil

1. In a medium bowl, whisk together vinegar, sugar, and chopped jalapeño.

2. Halve the cucumber lengthwise; remove seeds. Slice seeded cucumber very thinly into half-moons. Combine with dressing, drizzle in sesame oil, and toss to coat.

3. Marinate for at least 10 minutes before serving.

PER SERVING

Calories: 18 — Fat: 0g — Sodium: 1mg — Fiber: 0g

Carbohydrates: 4g — Sugar: 2g — Protein: 0g

STRAWBERRY, WALNUT, AND FLAXSEED SALAD

SERVES 2

Adding a beautiful appearance, a nutty flavor, and a delicious crunch to your salads, flaxseed is a good source of plant-based protein and also contributes essential fats (omega-3s) to your favorite foods. You can top salads, pastas, entrées, and even sandwiches with these delicious and nutritious seeds. This recipe uses flaxseed meal, which is made of ground flaxseed and makes it easier for your body to absorb the nutrients.

INGREDIENTS

4 cups strawberries, tops removed and quartered

1 cup crushed walnuts

2 tablespoons flaxseed meal

1 tablespoon red wine vinegar

$\frac{1}{2}$ tablespoon agave nectar

2 sprigs mint leaves

1. Add strawberries, walnuts, and flaxseed meal to a large bowl.

2. Drizzle vinegar and agave over the salad and toss to coat.

3. Split the salad between two salad bowls, garnish each with a mint sprig, and serve.

PER SERVING

Calories: 400 – Fat: 28g – Sodium: 3mg – Fiber: 10g

Carbohydrates: 33g – Sugar: 17g – Protein: 10g

CAESAR SALAD
SERVES 8

Without anchovies, the small fish traditionally used in Caesar dressing, this take on America's favorite salad fits perfectly in a plant-based diet. The taste is authentic as is, but for an additional dimension, top the salad with vegetarian Worcestershire sauce if you'd like.

INGREDIENTS

1 large egg yolk

1 tablespoon Dijon mustard

2 tablespoons lemon juice

2 medium cloves garlic, peeled and finely chopped

$\frac{1}{2}$ cup peanut oil

$\frac{1}{4}$ cup grated Parmigiano-Reggiano cheese

$\frac{1}{8}$ teaspoon cayenne pepper

$\frac{1}{8}$ teaspoon salt

$\frac{1}{8}$ teaspoon ground black pepper

1 medium head romaine lettuce, torn into bite-sized pieces

1 cup whole-wheat croutons

1 cup shaved Parmigiano-Reggiano cheese

1. In a medium bowl or food processor, combine egg yolk, mustard, lemon juice, and garlic. Vigorously whisk or process in the oil, starting with just a drop at a time and gradually drizzling it in a small stream until all is emulsified into a smooth mayonnaise. Stir in grated cheese, cayenne, salt, and black pepper.

2. Place the lettuce and croutons in a large bowl and toss with the dressing. Divide onto eight plates, arranging croutons on top. Sprinkle shaved cheese over each salad. Dressing may be made up to a week in advance.

PER SERVING

Calories: 196 – Fat: 19g – Sodium: 372mg – Fiber: 3g
Carbohydrates: 8g – Sugar: 2g – Protein: 7g

GRILLED VEGETABLE ANTIPASTO
SERVES 8

Although *antipasto* usually means "appetizer," no one's going to complain if you serve this as a side dish with your main meal. Some people prefer to remove the skin of the eggplant, but this is not a necessary step. When the semester starts to get hectic, roast extra vegetables while preparing this recipe, and you'll have healthy leftovers to incorporate into meals for the rest of the week; you can reheat them or serve cold.

INGREDIENTS

1 medium eggplant, cut into 16 wedges, lightly salted

2 medium yellow squash, quartered lengthwise

2 medium zucchini, quartered lengthwise

4 plum tomatoes, halved lengthwise

2 medium green bell peppers, halved and seeded

2 medium red bell peppers, halved and seeded

8 medium portobello mushrooms, stems removed

2 medium heads radicchio, core intact, quartered

2 tablespoons olive oil

$\frac{1}{8}$ teaspoon salt

$\frac{1}{8}$ teaspoon ground black pepper

$\frac{1}{8}$ teaspoon crushed red pepper

$\frac{1}{2}$ cup extra-virgin olive oil

1 tablespoon balsamic vinegar

$\frac{1}{8}$ teaspoon sugar

2 shallots, finely chopped

4 sprigs fresh thyme, leaves picked and chopped

8 sprigs parsley

1. Heat grill (or a stovetop grill pan) to medium-hot. In a large bowl, toss eggplant, squash, zucchini, tomatoes, peppers, mushrooms, and radicchio with olive oil, salt, pepper, and crushed red pepper.

2. Cook vegetables on the grill, without turning, until they are slightly more than halfway done. Eggplant and mushrooms will take longest, while the radicchio will take only a few minutes. Cook the tomatoes skin-side down only. Turn the other vegetables to finish, then arrange on a serving platter.

3. In a small bowl, whisk together extra-virgin olive oil, vinegar, sugar, shallots, and chopped thyme. Drizzle over cooked vegetables while they're still warm.

4. Marinate 20 minutes before serving, garnished with parsley sprigs.

PER SERVING
Calories: 229 — Fat: 17g — Sodium: 56mg — Fiber: 6g

Carbohydrates: 17g — Sugar: 10g — Protein: 5g

MIXED BABY GREENS WITH BALSAMIC VINAIGRETTE

SERVES 8

This is a nice, basic house salad. Stuff into a whole-wheat pita, or experiment with different greens, vinegars, and oils to change things up. Use good-quality vinegar and olive oil; they'll make a difference in this simple yet elegant dressing. (*Vinaigrette* is basically a sauce made of oil and vinegar, often dressed up with herbs and garlic or, in this recipe, shallots.)

INGREDIENTS

8 ounces mixed baby greens (mesclun)

2 ounces fresh chives, cut into 2" pieces

1 tablespoon balsamic vinegar

2 tablespoons extra-virgin olive oil

1 tablespoon finely chopped shallots

$\frac{1}{8}$ teaspoon salt

$\frac{1}{8}$ teaspoon ground black pepper

Wash greens and spin dry; combine with chives in a large bowl. In a small bowl, whisk together vinegar, oil, and shallots; season with salt and pepper. Add dressing to greens and toss well to coat.

PER SERVING

Calories: 39 – Fat: 3g – Sodium: 60mg – Fiber: 1g

Carbohydrates: 2g – Sugar: 1g – Protein: 1g

GARDEN SALAD WITH AVOCADO AND SPROUTS

SERVES 4

The avocado and sprouts make this a more nutritious version of the old standby garden salad. Avocados are ripe when they are slightly soft to the touch, like pears; save the rock-hard ones for a later day.

INGREDIENTS

1 tablespoon fresh lemon juice

3 tablespoons olive oil

1 tablespoon finely chopped fresh chives

$\frac{1}{2}$ teaspoon salt

$\frac{1}{4}$ teaspoon ground black pepper

2 medium heads Boston lettuce

2 medium ripe tomatoes, cored, cut into 8 wedges each

1 medium ripe avocado, peeled and pitted

1 cup alfalfa sprouts

1. Make the dressing: Combine lemon juice, olive oil, chives, salt, and pepper in a small bowl, mixing well.

2. Arrange lettuce leaves, stem-end in, onto four plates, making a flower petal pattern. Inner leaves will be too small, so reserve them for another use.

3. Toss tomatoes in 1 tablespoon dressing; place four tomato wedges on each salad. Cut avocado into eight wedges and toss with 1 tablespoon dressing; place two avocado wedges on each salad. Divide sprouts into four bunches and place a bunch in the center of each salad. Drizzle salads with remaining dressing or serve on the side.

PER SERVING

Calories: 170 — Fat: 15g — Sodium: 300mg — Fiber: 4g
Carbohydrates: 8g — Sugar: 3g — Protein: 3g

CHAPTER 5

SOUPS

Tomato Soup......................................114

Veggies and Rice Soup....................115

Cashew Cream
of Asparagus Soup..........................116

Barley Vegetable Soup....................117

Southwest Almond Soup................118

Vegetable Chowder..........................119

French Onion Soup..........................120

Gazpacho with Avocado.................121

Pumpkin Ale Soup...........................123

Minestrone with Pesto.....................124

Red Bean and Pasta Soup..............125

Smoky Black-Eyed Pea Soup
with Sweet Potatoes and Mustard
Greens...126

Smooth Cauliflower Soup
with Coriander..................................128

Spicy Sweet Potato Soup................129

Mushroom, Barley, and
Collard Greens Soup.......................130

Acorn Squash Soup with
Anise and Carrots............................131

Vegan Chili......................................132

Vegetable and Pasta Soup..............134

White Bean Soup with
Chipotle Croutons...........................135

Chickpea Soup.................................136

Red Lentil and
Sweet Potato Soup..........................137

Zucchini Soup..................................138

Green Onion Chive Soup................139

Cream of Carrot Soup
with Coconut...................................140

Tortilla Tomato Soup 141

TOMATO SOUP
SERVES 6

Tomato soup is a college comfort food classic. This recipe is not made with cream, but it has a smooth, rich taste you'll love. Top with a dollop of vegan sour cream or yogurt if you like.

INGREDIENTS

2 tablespoons olive oil

1 medium yellow onion, peeled and chopped

2 medium cloves garlic, peeled and finely chopped

4 pounds ripe tomatoes, peeled, seeded, and roughly chopped

1 teaspoon salt

1/4 teaspoon ground black pepper

1. In a large soup pot over medium heat, warm olive oil 1 minute. Add onion and garlic and cook 5–10 minutes until onions are translucent but not browned.

2. Stir in tomatoes and simmer 25–30 minutes until tomatoes are submerged in their own juices.

3. Transfer the mixture to a blender or food processor and purée until smooth. Season with salt and pepper. May be served hot or cold.

PER SERVING
Calories: 96 – Fat: 5g – Sodium: 401mg – Fiber: 4g
Carbohydrates: 12g – Sugar: 8g – Protein: 3g

Blender versus Food Processor
They seem interchangeable sometimes, but they're not. Blenders and food processors are different tools with different strengths. For ultra smooth purées, a blender is the first choice. For rougher purées, or chopping jobs with drier ingredients, use a processor.

VEGGIES AND RICE SOUP
SERVES 8

If you're cooking for just one or two, the batch size of this Veggies and Rice Soup recipe will leave you with plenty of leftovers for easy lunches or dinners through the school-week. To make this an even lighter soup with fewer calories, reduce the amount of brown rice you use.

INGREDIENTS

2 cups uncooked instant brown rice

4 cups California-blend vegetables, chopped

1 cup Brussels sprouts, cut in half

2 cups peeled and cubed sweet potatoes

4 cups Basic Vegetable Stock (see recipe in Chapter 8)

$\frac{1}{2}$ teaspoon all-purpose seasoning

1 medium clove garlic, minced

1 teaspoon Italian herbs

$\frac{1}{2}$ cup diced yellow onion

1 tablespoon olive oil

1 teaspoon dried oregano

$\frac{1}{4}$ cup fresh parsley

$\frac{1}{2}$ teaspoon ground black pepper

1 cup chopped celery

2 cups water

1. Combine all ingredients in a large saucepan. Cook on medium-high heat for 15 minutes.

2. Reduce heat to low and simmer for another 10 minutes. Add additional water if soup dries out.

PER SERVING

Calories: 271 – Fat: 3g – Sodium: 143mg – Fiber: 6g
Carbohydrates: 55g – Sugar: 7g – Protein: 6g

CASHEW CREAM OF ASPARAGUS SOUP

SERVES 4

A dairy-free and soy-free asparagus soup with a rich cashew base brings out the natural flavors of the asparagus without relying on other enhancers. Make sure you trim the bottom of the asparagus (check online for how-to tips; it's easy!) or clean it very well, as this portion of the vegetable often contains sand.

INGREDIENTS

1 medium white onion, peeled and chopped

4 medium cloves garlic, peeled and minced

2 tablespoons olive oil

2 pounds asparagus, trimmed and chopped

4 cups Basic Vegetable Stock (see recipe in Chapter 8)

$\frac{3}{4}$ cup raw cashews

$\frac{3}{4}$ cup water

$\frac{1}{4}$ teaspoon dried sage

$\frac{1}{2}$ teaspoon salt

$\frac{1}{4}$ teaspoon ground black pepper

2 teaspoons lemon juice

2 tablespoons nutritional yeast

1. In a large soup or stockpot, sauté onion and garlic in olive oil over medium heat for 2–3 minutes, until onion is soft. Reduce heat to low and carefully add asparagus and Basic Vegetable Stock.

2. Bring to a simmer, cover, and cook for 20 minutes. Cool slightly, then purée in a blender, working in batches as needed, until almost smooth. Return to pot over low heat.

3. In a food processor or blender, purée together cashews and water until smooth and add to soup. Add sage, salt, and pepper, and heat for a few more minutes, stirring to combine.

4. Stir in lemon juice and nutritional yeast just before serving.

PER SERVING

Calories: 273 – Fat: 18g – Sodium: 309mg – Fiber: 5g
Carbohydrates: 20g – Sugar: 7g – Protein: 10g

BARLEY VEGETABLE SOUP
SERVES 6

Barley and vegetable soup is an excellent "kitchen sink" recipe, meaning that you can toss in just about any fresh or frozen vegetables or spices you happen to have on hand for the perfect spur-of-the-moment plant-based meal.

INGREDIENTS

1 medium white onion, peeled and chopped

2 medium carrots, peeled and sliced

2 medium stalks celery, chopped

2 tablespoons olive oil

8 cups Basic Vegetable Stock (see recipe in Chapter 8)

1 cup barley

1½ cups frozen mixed vegetables

1 (14-ounce) can crushed tomatoes

½ teaspoon dried parsley

½ teaspoon dried thyme

2 bay leaves

⅛ teaspoon salt

⅛ teaspoon ground black pepper

1. In a large soup or stockpot, sauté onion, carrot, and celery in olive oil for 3–5 minutes, just until onions are almost soft.

2. Reduce heat to medium-low, and add remaining ingredients, except salt and pepper.

3. Bring to a simmer, cover, and allow to cook for at least 45 minutes, stirring occasionally.

4. Remove cover and allow to cook for 10 more minutes.

5. Remove bay leaves, season with salt and pepper.

PER SERVING
Calories: 234 – Fat: 5g – Sodium: 227mg – Fiber: 10g
Carbohydrates: 44g – Sugar: 8g – Protein: 6g

Varieties of Vegetable Broths
A basic vegetable broth is made by simmering vegetables, potatoes, and a bay leaf or two in water for at least 30 minutes (see recipe for Basic Vegetable Stock in Chapter 8). While you may be familiar with the canned and boxed stocks available at the grocery store, vegan chefs have a few other tricks up their sleeves to impart extra flavor to recipes calling for vegetable broth. Check your natural grocer for specialty flavored bouillon cubes such as vegetarian "chicken" or "beef" flavor, or shop the bulk bins for powdered vegetable broth mix.

SOUTHWEST ALMOND SOUP
SERVES 6

This soup is spicy, thick, and rich, with a wonderful texture and flavor combination. Since it's high in plant-based protein, Southwest Almond Soup can stand alone as a wonderful lunch. If your regular grocery store does not carry almond flour, try a health food store or order it online.

INGREDIENTS

3 tablespoons olive oil

1 medium white onion, peeled and chopped

2 medium cloves garlic, peeled and minced

1 medium jalapeño pepper, seeded and minced

3 tablespoons almond flour

1 teaspoon ground cumin

5 cups Basic Vegetable Stock (see recipe in Chapter 8)

$2/3$ cup creamy almond butter

$1/3$ cup unsweetened almond milk

$1/2$ teaspoon salt

$1/8$ teaspoon ground black pepper

$2/3$ cup sliced toasted almonds

$1/2$ cup Kale Pesto (see recipe in Chapter 8)

1. In a large soup pot, heat olive oil over medium heat. Add onion, garlic, and jalapeño; cook and stir for 5 minutes.

2. Add almond flour and cumin; cook for 1 minute. Then whisk in Basic Vegetable Stock and simmer for 2 minutes until thickened.

3. Add almond butter, almond milk, salt, and pepper. Simmer for 10 minutes until flavors are blended.

4. In a small bowl, combine almonds with Kale Pesto and mix. Serve soup with this mixture for topping.

PER SERVING

Calories: 374 – Fat: 32g – Sodium: 214mg – Fiber: 5g
Carbohydrates: 13g – Sugar: 4g – Protein: 10g

VEGETABLE CHOWDER
SERVES 8

Who says chowder has to have clams in it? This soup is what you make when it's cold outside and you don't want to trek to the dining hall. It's easy, filling, and delicious.

INGREDIENTS

3 tablespoons margarine

1 medium white onion, peeled and chopped

1 cup chopped celery

2 cups sliced carrots

$\frac{1}{2}$ cup water

3 cups Basic Vegetable Stock (see recipe in Chapter 8)

3 medium white potatoes, peeled and diced

3 cups skim milk

$\frac{1}{4}$ cup all-purpose flour

1. Melt margarine in a large, deep skillet over medium-high heat. Add onion, celery, and carrots and cook until tender, stirring occasionally. Add water, Basic Vegetable Stock, and potatoes; boil for 15 minutes or until potatoes are tender.

2. Add milk, stirring to combine, and turn heat down to medium. Add flour to thicken. If you need to thicken further, add more flour. Serve hot.

PER SERVING
Calories: 166 – Fat: 4g – Sodium: 127mg – Fiber: 3g
Carbohydrates: 26g – Sugar: 3g – Protein: 6g

Chowder for Everyone
Chowder is basically just a cream- or milk-based soup that you can enjoy a thousand different ways. Corn chowder is a popular variation, as is seafood chowder. This vegetable-packed recipe is a favorite of vegetarians and meat-eaters alike!

FRENCH ONION SOUP
SERVES 4

Vidalia onions are a sweet variety of onion that work particularly well in French Onion Soup. If you want more crunch in your soup, add some whole-wheat croutons for extra flavor and protein.

INGREDIENTS

1/4 cup olive oil

4 large Vidalia onions, peeled and sliced

4 medium cloves garlic, peeled and minced

1 tablespoon dried thyme

1/2 cup Worcestershire sauce

4 1/2 cups Basic Vegetable Stock (see recipe in Chapter 8)

1 teaspoon sea salt

1 teaspoon ground black pepper

4 slices whole-wheat French bread

4 ounces vegan mozzarella cheese

1. In a small sauté pan, heat olive oil over medium-high heat and cook onions until golden brown, about 3 minutes. Add garlic and sauté 1 minute.

2. In a 4-quart slow cooker, pour the sautéed vegetables, thyme, Worcestershire, Basic Vegetable Stock, salt, and pepper. Cover and cook on low heat 4 hours.

3. While the soup is cooking, preheat oven to the broiler setting. Lightly toast the slices of French bread.

4. To serve, ladle the soup into four broiler-safe bowls, place a slice of toasted French bread on top of each bowl, put a slice of cheese on top of the bread, and place the bowls under the broiler until the cheese has melted.

PER SERVING
Calories: 419 – Fat: 20g – Sodium: 1,145mg – Fiber: 6g
Carbohydrates: 55g – Sugar: 20g – Protein: 6g

GAZPACHO WITH AVOCADO
SERVES 6

This delicious gazpacho is a vegetable powerhouse. Because gazpacho is served cold, it's best enjoyed outside. Bring along a refreshing batch for a spring semester picnic on the college green with friends!

INGREDIENTS

2 medium cucumbers, peeled and diced

$\frac{1}{2}$ medium red onion, peeled and diced

2 large tomatoes, diced

$\frac{1}{4}$ cup chopped fresh cilantro

2 medium avocados, peeled, pitted, and diced

4 medium cloves garlic, peeled

2 tablespoons lime juice

1 tablespoon apple cider vinegar

$\frac{3}{4}$ cup Basic Vegetable Stock (see recipe in Chapter 8)

1 small jalapeño pepper, seeded and chopped

1 teaspoon salt

$\frac{1}{2}$ teaspoon ground black pepper

1. In a large bowl, mix together cucumbers, onion, tomatoes, cilantro, and avocados. Set half of the mixture aside. Place the other half in a food processor or blender and pulse to mix. Add garlic, lime juice, vinegar, Basic Vegetable Stock, and jalapeño and process until smooth.

2. Transfer the mixture to the bowl with the reserved cucumbers, onion, tomatoes, cilantro, and avocados. Stir gently to combine. Season with salt and pepper.

3. Chill in the refrigerator for at least 4 hours before serving.

PER SERVING
Calories: 114 — Fat: 6g — Sodium: 401mg — Fiber: 5g
Carbohydrates: 13g — Sugar: 5g — Protein: 2g

PUMPKIN ALE SOUP
SERVES 6

When processed pumpkin-flavored everything starts flooding the grocery stores, opt for this healthier plant-based soup option. It's perfect to get you through the fall semester. To make an alcohol-free version, eliminate the ale and add an extra cup of Basic Vegetable Stock. Garnish with extra thyme before serving.

INGREDIENTS

2 (15-ounce) cans pumpkin purée

$1/4$ cup diced white onion

2 medium cloves garlic, peeled and minced

2 teaspoons salt

1 teaspoon ground black pepper

$1/4$ teaspoon dried thyme

5 cups Basic Vegetable Stock (see recipe in Chapter 8)

1 (12-ounce) bottle pale ale beer

1. In a 4-quart slow cooker, add pumpkin purée, onion, garlic, salt, pepper, thyme, and Basic Vegetable Stock. Stir well. Cover and cook over low heat 4 hours. (If you don't have a slow cooker, heat a tablespoon of olive oil in a large soup pot over medium heat. Sauté the onion and garlic for 5 minutes. Add the rest of the ingredients except the beer, and simmer on medium-low heat for about 20 minutes. Then add the beer, if using, and simmer on low heat about 10 minutes more.)

2. Allow the soup to cool slightly, then process in a blender or with an immersion blender until smooth.

3. Pour the soup back into the slow cooker, add the beer, and cook 1 hour over low heat.

PER SERVING
Calories: 80 — Fat: 1g — Sodium: 789mg — Fiber: 4g
Carbohydrates: 16g — Sugar: 7g — Protein: 1g

MINESTRONE WITH PESTO
SERVES 12

It doesn't get much more plant-based than this. The Italian word *minestrone* translates roughly to "the big soup." It's a thick, hearty soup made with lots of vegetables, often with the addition of pasta or rice. If you can't find ditalini, you can substitute any small tubular pasta.

INGREDIENTS

1 tablespoon olive oil

2 medium stalks celery, cut into $\frac{1}{4}$" dice

1 large carrot, peeled and cut into $\frac{1}{4}$" dice

1 medium white potato, peeled and cut into $\frac{1}{4}$" dice

1 medium zucchini, cut into $\frac{1}{4}$" dice

1 medium yellow squash, cut into $\frac{1}{4}$" dice

1 large Spanish onion, peeled and cut into $\frac{1}{4}$" dice

2 medium leeks, washed and chopped (white parts only)

3 medium cloves garlic, peeled and finely chopped

1 teaspoon salt

1 teaspoon dried oregano

1 teaspoon dried thyme

1 bay leaf

2 quarts Basic Vegetable Stock (see recipe in Chapter 8)

1 (30-ounce) can diced tomatoes

2 cups cooked whole-wheat ditalini pasta

1 (14-ounce) can cannellini beans, drained and rinsed

$\frac{1}{8}$ teaspoon salt

$\frac{1}{8}$ teaspoon ground white pepper

4 tablespoons store-bought pesto

1. In a large soup pot or Dutch oven over medium-high heat, heat olive oil 1 minute. Add all diced vegetables, leeks, garlic, salt, oregano, thyme, and bay leaf. Cook 10–15 minutes until onions turn translucent. Add Basic Vegetable Stock and tomatoes. Bring to a full boil; reduce heat to a simmer and cook 45 minutes until potatoes are cooked through and tender.

2. Add cooked pasta and beans. Bring back to a boil and cook for 1 minute; season with salt and white pepper. Serve in bowls topped with a teaspoon of pesto.

PER SERVING
Calories: 201 – Fat: 4g – Sodium: 386mg – Fiber: 4g
Carbohydrates: 34g – Sugar: 6g – Protein: 8g

RED BEAN AND PASTA SOUP
SERVES 8

This is a hearty winter soup to warm up chilly nights. Serve it with a dollop of vegan sour cream atop each bowl of soup. For even more plant-based protein, choose a whole-wheat pasta option.

INGREDIENTS

1 medium yellow onion, peeled and chopped

3 medium cloves garlic, peeled and sliced

3 tablespoons olive oil

1 teaspoon dried oregano

2 bay leaves

1 (8-ounce) can tomato sauce

2 teaspoons salt

1 tablespoon soy sauce

1 (16-ounce) package dried red beans, soaked overnight in 1 quart cold water and drained

10 sprigs Italian parsley, including stems

6 cups Basic Vegetable Stock (see recipe in Chapter 8)

2 cups cooked whole-wheat orzo pasta

8 tablespoons vegan sour cream

1. In a pot large enough to hold all ingredients, cook onions and garlic with olive oil over medium heat for 5 minutes, until onions are translucent. Add oregano, bay leaves, tomato sauce, salt, and soy sauce. Bring to a simmer and add beans, parsley, and Basic Vegetable Stock.

2. Bring to a boil, then reduce to a low simmer and cook 90 minutes until beans are tender enough to mash between two fingers. In a blender, purée $\frac{1}{3}$ of the beans very well; add them back to the soup. Add cooked pasta and bring back to a boil for 1 minute more before serving garnished with sour cream.

PER SERVING
Calories: 339 — Fat: 8g — Sodium: 851mg — Fiber: 13g
Carbohydrates: 53g — Sugar: 4g — Protein: 16g

SMOKY BLACK-EYED PEA SOUP WITH SWEET POTATOES AND MUSTARD GREENS

SERVES 12

Black-eyed peas offer some of the delicious earthiness of green peas, but also a savory touch. Use any dark leafy greens you'd like, fresh or frozen, in place of the mustard greens. Thinly cut kale or collard greens are excellent choices and are equally antioxidant-rich.

INGREDIENTS

1 tablespoon olive oil

1 medium yellow onion, peeled and chopped

2 medium stalks celery, chopped

1 medium carrot, peeled and chopped

2 teaspoons plus $\frac{1}{8}$ teaspoon salt, divided

1 teaspoon dried thyme

2 teaspoons dried oregano

1 teaspoon ground cumin

1 dried chipotle chili, halved

2 bay leaves

1 pound dried black-eyed peas

2 quarts Basic Vegetable Stock (see recipe in Chapter 8)

1 large sweet potato, peeled and diced into 1" cubes

1 (10-ounce) package frozen mustard greens, chopped

1 (22-ounce) can diced tomatoes

$\frac{1}{8}$ teaspoon ground black pepper

2 cups corn bread croutons

$\frac{1}{3}$ cup chopped cilantro

1. In a large heavy-bottomed soup pot or Dutch oven over medium heat, heat oil 1 minute. Add onion, celery, carrot, and 2 teaspoons salt; cook 5 minutes until onions are translucent. Add thyme, oregano, cumin, chipotle chili, and bay leaves; cook 2 minutes more. Add black-eyed peas and Basic Vegetable Stock.

2. Bring to a boil, then simmer 2 hours until beans are very tender, adding Basic Vegetable Stock if necessary.

SMOKY BLACK-EYED PEA SOUP WITH SWEET POTATOES AND MUSTARD GREENS CONT.

3. Add sweet potatoes and cook 20 minutes more. Stir in chopped mustard greens and diced tomatoes. Cook 10 minutes more until potatoes and greens are tender. Adjust seasoning with remaining $1/8$ teaspoon salt and pepper, and consistency with additional Basic Vegetable Stock. The soup should be brothy. Serve garnished with corn bread croutons and a sprinkling of chopped cilantro.

PER SERVING

Calories: 104 — Fat: 2g — Sodium: 489mg — Fiber: 4g
Carbohydrates: 19g — Sugar: 5g — Protein: 3g

Using Smoked Chilies or Spices to Add Smoky Flavor
For a smoky flavor, nonvegetarian recipes often call for smoked pork bones or bacon. Vegetarians can achieve a similar result by adding smoked chilies such as chipotles (smoked jalapeños) to those dishes.

SMOOTH CAULIFLOWER SOUP WITH CORIANDER

SERVES 6

Here's another no-cream "cream soup." This soup is equally delicious hot or chilled. To make this recipe vegan, simply switch out the butter and milk for your favorite nondairy counterparts!

INGREDIENTS

2 tablespoons unsalted butter

1 medium yellow onion, peeled and chopped

1 medium head (about 2 pounds) cauliflower, cut into bite-sized pieces

2 cups Basic Vegetable Stock (see recipe in Chapter 8)

1 teaspoon salt

$\frac{1}{2}$ teaspoon ground white pepper

1 teaspoon ground coriander

$\frac{3}{4}$ cup cold 2% milk

2 tablespoons chopped parsley

1. In a large saucepan or soup pot over medium-high heat, melt butter. Add onion; cook until it is translucent but not brown, about 5 minutes. Add cauliflower; cook 1 minute. Add Basic Vegetable Stock, salt, pepper, and coriander; bring up to a rolling boil.

2. Reduce heat to medium and simmer until cauliflower is very tender, about 15 minutes. Transfer to a blender. Add half of the milk and purée until very smooth, scraping down the sides of the blender vase with a rubber spatula. Be very careful during this step, since hot liquids will splash out of blender if it is not started gradually (you may wish to purée in two batches, for safety). Transfer soup back to saucepan and thin with additional milk if necessary. Season; garnish with chopped parsley just before serving.

PER SERVING
Calories: 85 – Fat: 4g – Sodium: 437mg – Fiber: 2g
Carbohydrates: 9g – Sugar: 3g – Protein: 3g

SPICY SWEET POTATO SOUP
SERVES 4

Sweet potatoes have been found to retain most of their nutritional value through the process of baking or boiling, while it's been determined that steaming them undermines their formidable vitamin A levels. This recipe couldn't be simpler. If you don't have an immersion blender, allow the cooked sweet potatoes to cool slightly then purée in a regular blender (in batches if necessary).

INGREDIENTS

3 cups water

2 medium sweet potatoes, peeled and cut into $\frac{1}{4}$" slices

$\frac{1}{2}$ teaspoon cayenne pepper, divided

$\frac{1}{2}$ teaspoon salt, divided

1. In a medium pot over medium-high heat, add water and sweet potatoes and bring to a boil.

2. Reduce heat to simmer and cook until sweet potatoes are fork-tender, about 15 minutes. Remove from heat and reserve water from pot in a separate measuring cup.

3. Sprinkle sweet potatoes with $\frac{1}{4}$ teaspoon cayenne and $\frac{1}{4}$ teaspoon salt and add $\frac{1}{4}$ cup of removed water back to pot.

4. Using an immersion blender, emulsify potatoes, adding removed water as needed until desired thickness is achieved.

5. While emulsifying, add remaining cayenne and salt.

PER SERVING
Calories: 57 – Fat: 0g – Sodium: 310mg – Fiber: 2g
Carbohydrates: 14g – Sugar: 4g – Protein: 1g

MUSHROOM, BARLEY, AND COLLARD GREENS SOUP
SERVES 12

This should be called "Health Soup" for its concentration of cancer-fighting antioxidants, folate-rich greens, nourishing whole grains, and complete protein-forming combinations. If you haven't tried collards, you're in for a treat; they're a cousin to kale, which you could use instead of collards in this recipe if you'd like.

INGREDIENTS

2 tablespoons olive oil

2 pounds button mushrooms, chopped

1 large yellow onion, peeled and chopped

1 medium carrot, peeled and chopped

2 medium stalks celery, chopped

4 medium cloves garlic, peeled and roughly chopped

2 bay leaves

2 teaspoons dried oregano

$\frac{1}{2}$ teaspoon dried rosemary

2 teaspoons salt

$\frac{1}{2}$ teaspoon ground black pepper

2 cups pearl barley, rinsed

3 quarts Basic Vegetable Stock (see recipe in Chapter 8)

2 (10-ounce) packages frozen chopped collard greens

1. Heat oil in a large soup pot over medium-high heat for 1 minute. Add mushrooms, onions, carrot, celery, garlic, bay leaves, oregano, rosemary, salt, and pepper. Cook until vegetables have softened significantly and are stewing in their natural broth, about 15 minutes.

2. Stir in barley and Basic Vegetable Stock. Bring the soup up to a full boil, then reduce to a medium simmer and cook until barley is tender, about 40 minutes.

3. Add the collards; cook about 10 minutes more.

PER SERVING
Calories: 186 — Fat: 3g — Sodium: 435mg — Fiber: 8g
Carbohydrates: 36g — Sugar: 4g — Protein: 7g

ACORN SQUASH SOUP WITH ANISE AND CARROTS

SERVES 6

When the weather turns chilly, fall and winter squashes like acorn squash start showing up in the markets—just in time to make this smooth, soothing velvety soup. This soup might become your fall semester staple!

INGREDIENTS

1 tablespoon olive oil

2 medium yellow onions, peeled and chopped

1 teaspoon salt

1 medium acorn squash (about 2 pounds), peeled and cut into 1" chunks

2 large carrots, peeled and cut into 1" chunks

1 teaspoon anise seeds, toasted in a dry pan for 2 minutes until fragrant

$\frac{1}{4}$ cup cognac

1 pint Basic Vegetable Stock (see recipe in Chapter 8)

2 cups skim milk

2 tablespoons chopped fresh parsley

1. Heat the olive oil in a heavy medium saucepan over medium heat. Add the onions and salt; cook until translucent and slightly browned, about 10 minutes.

2. Lower heat to medium-low. Add the squash, carrots, and anise seeds; cook slowly, stirring the browned bits from the bottom of the pan frequently with a wooden spoon. These browned natural sugars will give the soup its caramelized complexity.

3. When the squash is soft and browned, add the cognac; cook 2 minutes to steam off the alcohol. Add the Basic Vegetable Stock; simmer 15 minutes.

4. In a blender, purée the soup with as much skim milk as necessary for a thick but soupy consistency. Garnish with chopped parsley.

PER SERVING

Calories: 121 – Fat: 3g – Sodium: 459mg – Fiber: 2g

Carbohydrates: 19g – Sugar: 3g – Protein: 5g

VEGAN CHILI
SERVES 8

This plant-based classic soup is sure to fill you up with healthy protein for classes, studying, and all your other activities throughout the day. Chili is all about the spice, and this version won't disappoint; several kinds of chilies provide plenty of heat, without the meat.

INGREDIENTS

1/4 cup olive oil

2 cups chopped yellow onion

1 cup chopped carrots

2 cups chopped assorted bell peppers

2 teaspoons salt

1 tablespoon chopped fresh garlic

2 small jalapeño peppers, seeded and chopped

1 tablespoon ground ancho chili pepper

1 chipotle in adobo, chopped

1 tablespoon toasted cumin seeds, ground

1 (28-ounce) can plum tomatoes, roughly chopped, juice included

1 (16-ounce) can red kidney beans, drained and rinsed

1 (16-ounce) can cannellini beans, drained and rinsed

1 (16-ounce) can black beans, drained and rinsed

1 cup tomato juice

1/4 cup finely chopped red onion

1/4 cup chopped fresh cilantro

1. Heat oil in a heavy-bottomed Dutch oven or large soup pot over medium heat. Add onions, carrots, bell peppers, and salt and cook 15 minutes until onions are soft.

2. Add garlic, jalapeños, ancho, chipotle, and cumin and cook 5 more minutes.

3. Stir in tomatoes, beans, and tomato juice. Simmer about 45 minutes. Serve with a garnish of red onions and cilantro.

PER SERVING
Calories: 256 – Fat: 7g – Sodium: 1,034mg – Fiber: 11g
Carbohydrates: 38g – Sugar: 8g – Protein: 11g

VEGETABLE AND PASTA SOUP
SERVES 6

To keep a quick and easy source of healthy vegetables on hand, grab a bag of frozen mixed vegetables at a wholesale store and keep them in your freezer for easier meal prepping. Use your favorite vegetables for this recipe—any and all will do!

INGREDIENTS

1 medium clove garlic, peeled and minced

1 cup diced red bell pepper

1 cup diced white onion

1 cup sliced celery

3 cups Basic Vegetable Stock (see recipe in Chapter 8)

4 cups frozen mixed vegetables

$\frac{1}{2}$ teaspoon all-purpose seasoning

$\frac{1}{4}$ cup chopped fresh parsley

1 cup diced baking potatoes

2 cups whole-wheat rotini pasta

2 cups water

1. Combine all ingredients in a large saucepan over medium-high heat. Cook 15 minutes.

2. Reduce heat to low and simmer another 10 minutes. Add additional water if soup dries out.

PER SERVING
Calories: 217 – Fat: 1g – Sodium: 181mg – Fiber: 11g
Carbohydrates: 46g – Sugar: 7g – Protein: 9g

WHITE BEAN SOUP WITH CHIPOTLE CROUTONS

SERVES 4

If you can find it, be sure to use the soy chorizo in this soup. It's tube shaped and packed in plastic; unwrap the "sausage" and sauté the crumbles until golden. Sprinkle them into the soup once it's hot.

INGREDIENTS

2 (15.5-ounce) cans cannellini beans, drained and rinsed

$1\frac{1}{2}$ cups fresh or canned tomatoes

1 teaspoon dried oregano

1 teaspoon chipotle sauce (adobo)

$\frac{1}{8}$ teaspoon salt

$\frac{1}{8}$ teaspoon ground black pepper

2 tablespoons olive oil (4 tablespoons if using soy chorizo)

1 (12-ounce) package soy chorizo "sausage"

1 cup garlic croutons sprinkled with ground chipotle chilies

2 tablespoons diced red onion

2 tablespoons chopped fresh cilantro

1. Put one can of the beans into a blender or food processor. Add tomatoes, oregano, chipotle sauce, salt, pepper, and 2 tablespoons olive oil and process until fairly smooth. Pour into a large saucepan.

2. If using the chorizo, heat 2 more tablespoons olive oil in a small skillet over medium-low heat and crumble and sauté the sausage.

3. Heat the soup in a saucepan over medium heat; stir in remaining beans and the chorizo "sausage." To serve, ladle soup into individual bowls and garnish with croutons, red onions, and cilantro.

PER SERVING

Calories: 494 — Fat: 24g — Sodium: 1,354mg — Fiber: 6g
Carbohydrates: 50g — Sugar: 5g — Protein: 23g

CHICKPEA SOUP
SERVES 6

This fragrant, delicious soup is great any time of year, but especially once the weather has turned colder. Enjoy during winter semester in your coziest library spot between study sessions!

INGREDIENTS

1 medium clove garlic, peeled and minced

1 cup diced bell pepper

1 cup diced yellow onion

3 teaspoons lemon juice

3 cups Basic Vegetable Stock (see recipe in Chapter 8)

$\frac{1}{2}$ teaspoon red pepper

1 teaspoon ground ginger

$\frac{1}{2}$ teaspoon ground cumin

4 cups cooked chickpeas

$\frac{1}{2}$ teaspoon all-purpose seasoning

2 cups sliced carrots

3 tablespoons tomato paste

1 cup cubed baking potatoes

1. Combine all ingredients in a large saucepan. Cook on medium-high heat for 15 minutes.

2. Simmer for another 10 minutes, then serve.

PER SERVING
Calories: 249 — Fat: 2g — Sodium: 224mg — Fiber: 11g
Carbohydrates: 46g — Sugar: 11g — Protein: 12g

RED LENTIL AND SWEET POTATO SOUP
SERVES 4

Plant-based proteins galore! For a creamier soup, add 1 cup of fat-free sour cream or nondairy yogurt after cooking. Swirl cream and soup together gently.

INGREDIENTS

1 medium white onion, peeled and chopped

1 medium stalk celery, finely chopped

1 large carrot, peeled and sliced

1½ cups cubed sweet potato

1 cup cooked red lentils

1 bay leaf

½ teaspoon minced fresh garlic

½ teaspoon all-purpose seasoning

5 cups Basic Vegetable Stock (see recipe in Chapter 8)

2 tablespoons chopped fresh cilantro

1. Spray a large saucepan with nonstick cooking spray. Add onions and celery and cook on medium-high heat for 2 minutes, stirring often.

2. Add carrots, sweet potatoes, lentils, bay leaf, garlic, all-purpose seasoning, and Basic Vegetable Stock to saucepan. Cover and cook on medium for 10 minutes.

3. Reduce heat to low and simmer for an additional 10 minutes. Remove bay leaf and blend soup in batches in a food processor or blender.

4. Return soup to saucepan, add cilantro, and simmer for 5 minutes.

PER SERVING
Calories: 129 – Fat: 0g – Sodium: 235mg – Fiber: 7g
Carbohydrates: 27g – Sugar: 6g – Protein: 6g

Plentiful Lentils
Lentils come in many colors, from yellow to red-orange to green, brown, and black. Lentils can come whole or split, and many varieties come decorticated, or with their skins removed. All varieties are high in protein, so they're a great choice all around for your plant-based diet!

ZUCCHINI SOUP
SERVES 8

This smooth and soothing blend of fresh herbs and spices is a unique option. To up the spice, add more cayenne pepper and paprika, if you prefer. Switch things up with this Zucchini Soup in the middle of the semester.

INGREDIENTS

4 cups sliced peeled zucchini

4 cups Basic Vegetable Stock (see recipe in Chapter 8)

4 medium cloves garlic, peeled and minced

2 tablespoons lime juice

2 teaspoons curry powder

1 teaspoon dried marjoram leaves

$\frac{1}{4}$ teaspoon celery seeds

$\frac{1}{2}$ cup canned full-fat coconut milk

$\frac{1}{4}$ teaspoon cayenne pepper

1 teaspoon paprika

1. Combine all ingredients except coconut milk, cayenne pepper, and paprika in a slow cooker, and cook on high for 3–4 hours.

2. Process the cooked zucchini mixture with coconut milk in a blender until combined.

3. Season with cayenne pepper. Sprinkle with paprika and serve warm.

PER SERVING
Calories: 46 – Fat: 3g – Sodium: 11mg – Fiber: 1g
Carbohydrates: 5g – Sugar: 2g – Protein: 1g

GREEN ONION CHIVE SOUP
SERVES 2

Chive adds a sweet, mild oniony taste to this lovely green soup. The plant-based protein in this soup will fuel your long study sessions and warm you up during the winter semester. You may have encountered edamame in a Japanese restaurant, where these soybeans are often served in their shells as an appetizer.

INGREDIENTS

3 teaspoons olive oil

$\frac{1}{2}$ cup shredded zucchini

$\frac{1}{2}$ cup chopped shallots

1 medium clove garlic, peeled and minced

1 cup frozen shelled edamame, thawed

1 cup chopped green onion

$\frac{1}{2}$ cup chopped fresh chives

2 cups Basic Vegetable Stock (see recipe in Chapter 8)

$\frac{1}{2}$ cup water

1. Heat olive oil in a large soup pot or Dutch oven over medium-low heat. Sauté zucchini, shallots, and garlic in oil for 3–5 minutes. Add edamame, green onions, and chives and cook for 2 minutes more.

2. Add Basic Vegetable Stock and water. Increase heat to high and bring to a boil. Reduce heat to low and simmer for 5 minutes.

3. In batches, purée soup in a blender or food processor.

PER SERVING
Calories: 221 — Fat: 10g — Sodium: 38mg — Fiber: 9g

Carbohydrates: 22g — Sugar: 7g — Protein: 13g

Chive As Insect Repellent
Chive has such a strong scent that it can be used in gardens as an insect repellent. Garlic has also been known to be an effective defense against pests.

CREAM OF CARROT SOUP WITH COCONUT
SERVES 6

The addition of coconut milk transforms an ordinary carrot and ginger soup into a heavenly dish. The sweet and spicy flavors combined with the vegan ingredients perfect this plant-based soup. Surprise your roommates with this unexpected treat!

INGREDIENTS

3 medium carrots, peeled and chopped

1 large sweet potato, peeled and chopped

1 medium yellow onion, peeled and chopped

3½ cups Basic Vegetable Stock (see recipe in Chapter 8)

3 medium cloves garlic, peeled and minced

2 teaspoons minced fresh ginger

1 (14-ounce) can coconut milk

1 teaspoon salt

¾ teaspoon ground cinnamon

1. In a large soup or stockpot, bring carrots, sweet potato, and onion to a simmer in the Basic Vegetable Stock. Add garlic and ginger, cover, and heat for 20–25 minutes, until carrots and potatoes are soft.

2. Allow to cool slightly, then transfer to a blender and purée until smooth.

3. Return soup to pot. Over very low heat, stir in milk and salt, stirring well to combine. Heat just until heated through, another 3–4 minutes.

4. Garnish with cinnamon just before serving.

PER SERVING
Calories: 184 – Fat: 13g – Sodium: 433mg – Fiber: 2g
Carbohydrates: 15g – Sugar: 5g – Protein: 3g

Eat Carrots for Your Eyes
In addition to being crunchy and tasty, carrots are also really good for you. They're rich in dietary fiber, antioxidants, and minerals, as well as vitamin A, which helps maintain your vision. An urban legend says that eating large amounts of carrots will allow you to see in the dark! While this isn't exactly true, you should still try to work more carrots into your diet; with the amount of screen time you put in, your eyes deserve all the help they can get.

TORTILLA TOMATO SOUP
SERVES 8

This soup is a fun alternative to tacos with the same great flavors. You might also add a dollop of fat-free or vegan sour cream for a cool, creamy taste. To up the spice in this soup, add hot sauce as you see fit.

INGREDIENTS

$\frac{1}{2}$ cup diced red onion

1 medium clove garlic, peeled and minced

$\frac{1}{2}$ teaspoon all-purpose seasoning

4 cups diced tomatoes

3 cups crushed tomatoes

$\frac{1}{4}$ teaspoon ground black pepper

$\frac{1}{4}$ cup chopped fresh cilantro

3 cups Basic Vegetable Stock (see recipe in Chapter 8)

3 cups whole-wheat tortilla strips

$\frac{1}{2}$ cup shredded Cheddar cheese

1. Combine all ingredients except tortillas and cheese in a large saucepan. Cook on medium-high heat for 15 minutes. Reduce heat to low and simmer for another 10 minutes.

2. Toast tortilla strips in toaster oven until crispy.

3. Serve soup and sprinkle with cheese and tortilla strips.

PER SERVING
Calories: 184 – Fat: 7g – Sodium: 405mg – Fiber: 3g
Carbohydrates: 27g – Sugar: 8g – Protein: 4g

Slow Down!
Did you know that it takes your stomach about 20 minutes to let your brain know it's full? For this reason, it's important for you to slow down and give your body a chance to do its job. Chew each bite slowly, savor the taste of your food, and stop when your brain says "enough"!

CHAPTER 6

MAIN DISHES

Spicy Edamame and Tofu Ramen.....144

Spanish Artichoke
and Zucchini Paella............................145

Veggie-Stuffed Peppers....................146

Manchego and Potato Tacos
with Pickled Jalapeños.....................147

Pesto Pizza...149

Sun-Dried Tomato Risotto
with Spinach and Pine Nuts.............150

Baked Ziti...151

Portobello and Pepper Fajitas.......152

"Macaroni and Cheese"
with Spinach and Tomatoes............153

Easy Pad Thai Noodles 154

Pinto Burrito Bowl.............................156

Sweet Potato and Rosemary Pizza..157

Easy Eggplant Parmigiana 158

Spinach and Feta Pie.......................159

Easiest Black Bean Burger
Recipe in the World..........................161

Chickpea Soft Tacos.........................162

Orecchiette with Roasted Peppers,
Green Beans, and Pesto 163

Garden Quesadillas 164

Vegan Stroganoff...............................166

Veggie-Stuffed Zucchini 167

Spaghetti with Sweet Corn, Tomatoes,
and Goat Cheese...............................168

"Chorizo" Rice Bowl 169

Seitan Buffalo Wings 171

Barbecue Tempeh Pizza...................172

Edamame Pad Thai 173

SPICY EDAMAME AND TOFU RAMEN
SERVES 4

Ditch the college classic ramen packets, which are highly processed and packed with sodium, and go for this Spicy Edamame and Tofu Ramen. It's flavored with vegetable broth, mushroom broth, miso, soy sauce, and sriracha, with tofu and edamame bringing the protein to the party. Look for sriracha, a hot pepper sauce, in the supermarket condiment aisle.

INGREDIENTS

1/2 ounce (14 grams) dried shiitake mushrooms

1 tablespoon sesame oil

4 large cloves garlic, peeled and finely chopped

1 quart Basic Vegetable Stock (see recipe in Chapter 8)

3 tablespoons red miso paste

1/4 cup soy sauce

2 teaspoons sriracha

10 ounces brown rice ramen noodles

3 ounces bok choy, roughly chopped

1 cup organic shelled edamame

4 ounces extra-firm organic tofu, diced into small squares

2 small green onions, thinly sliced

1. Add dried mushrooms to a medium bowl and cover with boiling water. Let sit 20 minutes.

2. In a large pot, heat sesame oil on medium-low. Add garlic and cook 1 minute, stirring occasionally. Add Basic Vegetable Stock, miso paste, soy sauce, sriracha, and soaked mushrooms along with their liquid, and bring to a boil. Reduce to a simmer and cook 15 minutes. While broth is cooking, prepare noodles according to package directions.

3. Add bok choy and edamame to broth and cook an additional 5 minutes.

4. To serve, add noodles to a bowl and cover with broth. Top with tofu squares and green onions and serve immediately.

PER SERVING
Calories: 428 – Fat: 10g – Sodium: 1,503mg – Fiber: 9g
Carbohydrates: 63g – Sugar: 4g – Protein: 19g

SPANISH ARTICHOKE AND ZUCCHINI PAELLA

SERVES 4

Traditional Spanish paellas are always cooked with saffron (a spice known for its bright color and high price), but this version with zucchini, artichokes, and bell peppers uses turmeric instead for the same golden hue. Experiment with different types of squashes to switch things up even more.

INGREDIENTS

3 medium cloves garlic, peeled and minced

1 medium yellow onion, peeled and diced

2 tablespoons olive oil

1 cup uncooked brown rice

1 (15-ounce) can crushed tomatoes

1 medium green bell pepper, seeded and chopped

1 medium red bell pepper, seeded and chopped

$\frac{1}{2}$ cup chopped artichoke hearts

2 medium zucchini, sliced

2 cups Basic Vegetable Stock (see recipe in Chapter 8)

1 tablespoon paprika

$\frac{1}{2}$ teaspoon turmeric

$\frac{3}{4}$ teaspoon dried parsley

$\frac{1}{2}$ teaspoon salt

1. In the largest skillet you can find, heat garlic and onions in olive oil over medium heat for 3–4 minutes, until onions are almost soft. Add rice, stirring well to coat, and heat for another minute, stirring to prevent burning.

2. Add tomatoes, bell peppers, artichokes, and zucchini, stirring to combine. Add Basic Vegetable Stock and remaining ingredients, cover, and simmer for 15–20 minutes or until rice is done.

PER SERVING

Calories: 329 – Fat: 8g – Sodium: 517mg – Fiber: 8g
Carbohydrates: 58g – Sugar: 11g – Protein: 8g

VEGGIE-STUFFED PEPPERS
SERVES 4

Perfect for your next dorm potluck! When you place the peppers on the baking pan, add a little water to the pan so that the peppers don't burn. Add brown rice to the stuffed peppers, if you prefer.

INGREDIENTS

4 large green bell peppers

6 cups water

1 (15-ounce) can pinto beans, drained and rinsed

2 cups whole kernel corn

$3/4$ cup shredded Cheddar cheese

$1/2$ tablespoon vegetable oil

1 medium clove garlic, peeled and crushed

$1/2$ medium yellow onion, peeled and chopped

1 teaspoon ground black pepper

1. Preheat oven to 375°F.

2. Cut off the tops of the green peppers. Remove the seeds.

3. In a large deep saucepan, boil water; add peppers and cook for 5 minutes. Remove peppers; place upside down on a paper towel to drain.

4. Mix all remaining ingredients in a medium bowl. Divide ingredients evenly among peppers and stuff them. Place peppers in a baking dish, filled-side up; bake about 20 minutes. Serve hot.

PER SERVING
Calories: 269 — Fat: 8g — Sodium: 288mg — Fiber: 5g
Carbohydrates: 37g — Sugar: 9g — Protein: 14g

No Meat?
Stuffed peppers is another meal that is traditionally made with meat but doesn't have to be. In fact, there are lots of varieties, some including rice, others including bread crumbs, and so on. If you're vegetarian or simply looking for a lighter meal, you'll find that a meatless version can be just as satisfying.

MANCHEGO AND POTATO TACOS WITH PICKLED JALAPEÑOS

SERVES 8

Right from the package, corn tortillas are cardboardy and mealy, and flour tortillas are tough like leather. Both should be exposed to either dry or moist heat for 1 minute before serving. You'll notice a definite "puff" in most tortillas when they're properly softened.

INGREDIENTS

1 cup leftover mashed potatoes

8 (6") soft corn tortillas

$\frac{1}{4}$ pound Manchego cheese, cut into 16 small sticks

16 slices pickled jalapeño pepper (available in Mexican sections and ethnic specialty stores)

4 tablespoons unsalted butter, divided

1. Spoon 1 tablespoon of mashed potato into the center of each tortilla. Flatten out the potatoes, leaving a 1" border. Lay two pieces of Manchego and two pieces pickled jalapeño onto each tortilla, then fold closed into a half-moon shape.

2. In a large skillet over medium heat, melt half of the butter. Gently lay four tacos into the pan, and cook until nicely browned, about 3–4 minutes on each side. Drain on paper towels. Repeat with remaining tacos and remaining butter. Snip tacos in half before serving with salsa.

PER SERVING

Calories: 178 – Fat: 10g – Sodium: 249mg – Fiber: 2g
Carbohydrates: 16g – Sugar: 1g – Protein: 5g

PESTO PIZZA
SERVES 2

While the college lifestyle can sometimes lead to unhealthy eating habits, you can rest assured with this Pesto Pizza that you are making a nutritious choice. Instead of loading up on carbs with traditional pizza dough, this recipe uses a whole-wheat pita pocket for a protein boost. Garnish with fresh basil before serving.

INGREDIENTS

3 tablespoons jarred basil and tomato pesto sauce

1 (6") whole-wheat pita pocket bread

4 button mushrooms, sliced

$\frac{1}{3}$ cup grated mozzarella cheese

1. Spread pesto sauce on pita pocket. Lay mushroom slices on the sauce. Sprinkle cheese on top.

2. Place pita pocket on a microwave-safe plate or a paper towel. Microwave on high heat for 3–5 minutes, until the cheese melts. Serve.

PER SERVING

Calories: 257 – Fat: 13g – Sodium: 554mg – Fiber: 3g
Carbohydrates: 24g – Sugar: 3g – Protein: 10g

SUN-DRIED TOMATO RISOTTO WITH SPINACH AND PINE NUTS

SERVES 4

Risotto is a creamy rice dish usually made with a high-starch variety of white rice such as Arborio, but a short-grain brown rice can also be used to good effect. If you're using dehydrated tomatoes, rehydrate them first by covering in water for at least 10 minutes, and add the soaking water to the broth. If you're using tomatoes packed in oil, add 2 tablespoons of the oil to risotto at the end of cooking, instead of the vegan margarine.

INGREDIENTS

1 medium yellow onion, peeled and diced

4 medium cloves garlic, peeled and minced

2 tablespoons olive oil

1½ cups short-grain brown rice

6 cups Basic Vegetable Stock (see recipe in Chapter 8), divided

⅔ cup rehydrated sun-dried tomatoes, sliced

½ cup fresh spinach leaves

1 tablespoon chopped fresh basil

2 tablespoons vegan margarine

2 tablespoons nutritional yeast

⅛ teaspoon salt

⅛ teaspoon ground black pepper

¼ cup pine nuts

1. In a large saucepan, heat onion and garlic in olive oil over medium heat until just soft, about 2–3 minutes. Add rice and toast for 1 minute, stirring constantly.

2. Add ¾ cup Basic Vegetable Stock and stir to combine. When most of the liquid has been absorbed, add another ½ cup, stirring constantly. Continue adding Basic Vegetable Stock ½ cup at a time until rice is cooked, about 20 minutes.

3. Add another ½ cup Basic Vegetable Stock, tomatoes, and spinach and reduce heat to low. Stir to combine well. Heat for 3–4 minutes, until tomatoes are soft and spinach is wilted.

4. Stir in basil, margarine, and nutritional yeast. Taste, then season lightly with a bit of salt and pepper.

5. Allow to cool slightly, then top with pine nuts. Risotto will thicken a bit as it cools.

PER SERVING
Calories: 454 – Fat: 16g – Sodium: 158mg – Fiber: 5g
Carbohydrates: 68g – Sugar: 6g – Protein: 9g

BAKED ZITI
SERVES 10

Italian Americans have a cuisine that is distinctly their own, based on an adaptation of ingredients available to their immigrant ancestors when they arrived in the United States. Many staple dishes of the Italian-American table, such as this classic Baked Ziti, can be go-to dishes in a plant-based diet.

INGREDIENTS

1 pound uncooked whole-wheat ziti

$\frac{1}{2}$ teaspoon olive oil

1 quart tomato sauce, divided

1 pound part-skim ricotta cheese

1 pound part-skim mozzarella cheese, shredded

1 tablespoon chopped fresh Italian parsley

Where to Find Vegan Cheese

If you don't eat dairy, you might be wondering where you can find some vegan cheese. Most major grocery stores carry Daiya, but Whole Foods is often a good source for nondairy cheese. The Kite Hill brand makes a delicious almond milk ricotta.

1. Prepare ziti al dente (still a little chewy) according to package directions; drain, rinse, and toss with olive oil.

2. Preheat oven to 350°F.

3. Line the bottom of a 9" × 13" baking pan with half of the tomato sauce. Distribute half of the cooked ziti into the pan. Distribute ricotta by the tablespoonful onto the ziti and then sprinkle on half of the shredded cheese. Layer on remaining ziti. Cover the top with most of remaining sauce, saving about $\frac{1}{2}$ cup for later—the top layer does not need to be even—or use all remaining sauce to cover the pasta completely. Sprinkle on remaining shredded cheese.

4. Bake 25 minutes until cheese is bubbly and starting to brown. Serve with additional tomato sauce on the side and garnish with chopped parsley.

PER SERVING
Calories: 348 – Fat: 12g – Sodium: 790mg – Fiber: 7g
Carbohydrates: 38g – Sugar: 5g – Protein: 24g

PORTOBELLO AND PEPPER FAJITAS

SERVES 2

Fajitas are fun! Although onions and peppers are the most traditional sort of vegetables used to make them, you can grill up any sort of produce to go with these. Serve with nondairy sour cream, if you like.

INGREDIENTS

2 tablespoons olive oil

2 large portobello mushrooms, cut into strips

1 medium green bell pepper, seeded and cut into strips

1 medium red bell pepper, seeded and cut into strips

1 medium yellow onion, peeled and cut into strips

¾ teaspoon chili powder

¼ teaspoon ground cumin

⅛ teaspoon hot sauce

1 tablespoon chopped fresh cilantro

2 (12") whole-wheat tortillas, warmed

1. Heat olive oil in a large skillet over medium heat and add mushrooms, bell peppers, and onion. Allow to cook for 3–5 minutes until vegetables are almost done.

2. Add chili powder, cumin, and hot sauce, and stir to combine. Cook for 2–3 minutes until mushrooms and peppers are soft. Remove from heat and stir in fresh cilantro.

3. Spread half the mushroom and pepper mixture in the middle of each tortilla, fold in half, and serve.

PER SERVING

Calories: 491 – Fat: 22g – Sodium: 381mg – Fiber: 11g
Carbohydrates: 66g – Sugar: 10g – Protein: 12g

"MACARONI AND CHEESE" WITH SPINACH AND TOMATOES

SERVES 2

Mac and cheese is a college classic. Opt for this healthier version without the refined, white-wheat pasta. This lentil pasta is protein-filled, and the "cheese" used here is completely dairy-free and vegan, with added protein from the cashews.

INGREDIENTS

2 cups uncooked lentil rotini pasta

2 tablespoons olive oil, divided

2 cups fresh spinach leaves

$\frac{1}{2}$ cup raw unsalted cashews

4 medium cloves garlic, peeled and finely chopped

$\frac{1}{2}$ cup plus 2 tablespoons water

$\frac{1}{2}$ teaspoon salt

$\frac{1}{2}$ teaspoon ground black pepper

$\frac{1}{2}$ cup halved cherry tomatoes

1. Prepare pasta according to package directions. Rinse and drain.

2. In a medium saucepan, heat 1 tablespoon olive oil on medium-low. Add spinach leaves and cook 1–2 minutes until wilted. Remove from heat.

3. In a blender or food processor, blend together cashews, garlic, water, remaining tablespoon olive oil, salt, and pepper on high speed until completely smooth, about 10–20 seconds.

4. Return pasta to pot and add sauce. Mix together on low heat; cook about 2–3 minutes until sauce is warm and thick. Fold in spinach and tomatoes, and serve warm.

PER SERVING

Calories: 697 – Fat: 30g – Sodium: 611mg – Fiber: 15g
Carbohydrates: 83g – Sugar: 5g – Protein: 34g

EASY PAD THAI NOODLES
SERVES 6

This simple and quick dish uses the flavors and textures of Southeast Asia in a recipe perfect for a late-night dinner after evening classes, or separated into containers for your weekly meal-prepping.

INGREDIENTS

1 pound uncooked thin brown rice noodles

1/4 cup tahini

1/4 cup ketchup

1/4 cup soy sauce

2 tablespoons rice vinegar

3 tablespoons lime juice

2 tablespoons sugar

3/4 teaspoon crushed red pepper flakes

1 (14-ounce) block firm tofu, diced

3 medium cloves garlic, peeled and chopped

1/4 cup vegetable oil

4 medium green onions, chopped

1/2 teaspoon salt

1/4 cup chopped peanuts

1. In a small bowl, cover noodles in hot water and set aside to soak until soft, about 5 minutes.

2. In a separate small bowl, whisk together tahini, ketchup, soy sauce, vinegar, lime juice, sugar, and red pepper flakes. Set aside.

3. In a large skillet over medium-high heat, fry tofu and garlic in oil until tofu is golden brown. Add drained noodles, stirring to combine well, and fry 2–3 minutes.

4. Reduce heat to medium and add the tahini mixture, stirring well to combine. Allow to cook 3–4 minutes until well combined and heated through.

5. Add green onions and salt and heat 1 more minute, stirring well. Sprinkle with peanuts and serve.

PER SERVING

Calories: 544 – Fat: 21g – Sodium: 905mg – Fiber: 5g
Carbohydrates: 74g – Sugar: 9g – Protein: 15g

PINTO BURRITO BOWL
SERVES 2

Burritos aren't exactly considered health foods, but if you consider all the plant-based ingredients—the beans and vegetables—that are typically found inside a burrito, you may start to think of burritos in a different way. If you like spicy, this bowl tastes especially good drizzled with hot sauce.

INGREDIENTS

1 tablespoon olive oil

4 medium cloves garlic, peeled and minced

$\frac{1}{2}$ cup uncooked brown rice

$1\frac{1}{4}$ cups Basic Vegetable Stock (see recipe in Chapter 8)

$\frac{1}{2}$ cup diced tomatoes

$\frac{1}{2}$ teaspoon ground cumin

$\frac{1}{4}$ teaspoon salt

2 tablespoons chopped fresh cilantro, divided

2 cups chopped romaine lettuce

1 (15-ounce) can pinto beans, drained and rinsed

1 cup cooked yellow corn kernels

$\frac{1}{2}$ cup chopped cherry tomatoes

$\frac{1}{2}$ large ripe avocado, peeled, pitted, and sliced

2 tablespoons fresh lime juice

1. Heat oil in a medium pot on medium-low. Add garlic and cook 1 minute. Add rice, Basic Vegetable Stock, tomatoes, cumin, and salt. Bring to a boil, reduce to a simmer, and cover; cook about 30 minutes or until liquid is absorbed and rice is fluffy. When rice is finished cooking, stir in 1 tablespoon cilantro.

2. Add lettuce to a serving bowl. Top with the rice mixture, beans, corn, tomatoes, and avocado. Top off with lime juice and remaining cilantro, and serve warm.

PER SERVING
Calories: 556 – Fat: 14g – Sodium: 592mg – Fiber: 8g
Carbohydrates: 92g – Sugar: 7g – Protein: 18g

SWEET POTATO AND ROSEMARY PIZZA
SERVES 6

You won't find this plant-based authentic Italian dish at the campus pizza joint. Simple four- or five-ingredient pizzas like this one perfume street corners in some parts of Rome.

INGREDIENTS

1 (14-ounce) can prepared pizza crust dough

$1\frac{1}{2}$ tablespoons olive oil, divided

1 large sweet potato, peeled

1 teaspoon dried rosemary

$\frac{1}{8}$ teaspoon salt

$\frac{1}{8}$ teaspoon ground black pepper

1. Preheat oven to 400°F. Spread dough to $\frac{1}{4}$" thickness onto a doubled-up, lightly greased sheet pan. Brush on a light coating of olive oil.

2. Shred the sweet potato into a $\frac{1}{4}$"-thick layer over the pizza crust using the large-holed side of a box grater. Distribute rosemary evenly on top of potato. Sprinkle remaining olive oil over the pizza and season it with salt and pepper.

3. Bake 20–25 minutes until potato is cooked through and begins to brown.

PER SERVING
Calories: 220 – Fat: 5g – Sodium: 445mg – Fiber: 2g
Carbohydrates: 38g – Sugar: 6g – Protein: 6g

What Is a Doubled-Up Sheet Pan?
To buffer baking foods from the direct heat of oven elements, chefs often stack two identical baking sheets (known in the industry as "sheet pans") together, creating an air pocket that protects food from burning on the bottom. Commercially manufactured pans, such as Baker's Secret pans, incorporate this concept into their insulated bakeware.

EASY EGGPLANT PARMIGIANA
SERVES 4

Opt for freshly grated Parmigiano-Reggiano cheese for a more authentic flavor. Serve alongside whole-wheat pasta for the perfect plant-based dinner on a busy school-night.

INGREDIENTS

1 medium eggplant, peeled

$\frac{1}{2}$ teaspoon dried basil

$\frac{1}{2}$ teaspoon dried oregano

$\frac{1}{8}$ teaspoon garlic salt

1 cup spaghetti sauce

4 slices mozzarella cheese

$\frac{1}{4}$ cup grated Parmesan cheese

1. Preheat oven to 350°F. Spray an 8" × 8" baking pan with nonstick cooking spray.

2. Wash eggplant and cut into slices about $\frac{1}{4}$" thick. Stir basil, oregano, and garlic salt into spaghetti sauce.

3. Lay out half the eggplant slices flat on the prepared baking pan. Spoon the spaghetti sauce over the top. Cover the eggplant with foil and bake for 20 minutes or until tender. Remove from the oven. Uncover and lay the mozzarella slices on top.

4. Bake another 3–5 minutes, until the cheese melts. Sprinkle with Parmesan cheese and serve.

PER SERVING
Calories: 152 — Fat: 7g — Sodium: 510mg — Fiber: 5g
Carbohydrates: 12g — Sugar: 8g — Protein: 9g

SPINACH AND FETA PIE

SERVES 8

Every June on Manhattan's Ninth Avenue, there's an international food festival. The owners of a Greek bakery feature a spinach and feta pie like this one. You can decorate this pie with tomatoes if desired.

INGREDIENTS

4 cups fresh spinach leaves

3 tablespoons olive oil

1 medium yellow onion, peeled and chopped

1 cup grated Swiss cheese

2 large eggs

$1\frac{1}{4}$ cups light cream

$\frac{1}{4}$ teaspoon salt

$\frac{1}{4}$ teaspoon ground black pepper

$\frac{1}{8}$ teaspoon ground nutmeg

$\frac{1}{4}$ cup grated Parmesan cheese

1 (10") deep-dish pie crust, prebaked 5 minutes at 375°F

6 ounces feta cheese, crumbled

2 medium tomatoes, sliced

1. Preheat oven to 350°F. Wash and stem spinach; steam in a medium saucepan until wilted. Squeeze out excess water and chop. Heat the olive oil in a small skillet over medium heat, and cook onion until golden, about 7 minutes; toss with the spinach. Stir in Swiss cheese.

2. Combine eggs, cream, salt, pepper, nutmeg, and Parmesan cheese in a blender. Blend 1 minute. Spread the spinach mixture into the crust. Pour on the egg mixture, pressing through with your fingers to make sure it soaks through to the crust. Sprinkle feta cheese on egg mixture and arrange tomato slices on top.

3. Bake 45 minutes, until a knife inserted in the pie comes out clean. Serve hot or room temperature.

PER SERVING

Calories: 399 – Fat: 29g – Sodium: 464mg – Fiber: 2g

Carbohydrates: 19g – Sugar: 4g – Protein: 13g

EASIEST BLACK BEAN BURGER RECIPE IN THE WORLD

SERVES 6

These easy-to-prepare black bean burgers can help satisfy those cravings when you want to stick with plant-based proteins but also want to take a big bite out of something "meaty." Serve with lettuce and tomato and enjoy!

INGREDIENTS

1 (15-ounce) can black beans, drained

3 tablespoons minced white onion

1 teaspoon salt

1 1/2 teaspoons garlic powder

2 teaspoons dried parsley

1 teaspoon chili powder

2/3 cup all-purpose flour

1/4 cup oil, for pan-frying

1. In a blender or food processor, process the black beans until halfway mashed, or mash with a fork. Transfer beans to a medium bowl.

2. Add minced onions, salt, garlic powder, parsley, and chili powder, and mash to combine.

3. Add flour, a bit at a time, mashing together to combine. You may need a little bit more or less than 2/3 cup flour. Beans should stick together completely. Form into six patties.

4. In a medium skillet over medium heat, warm the oil. Add the patties and pan-fry 2–3 minutes on each side. Patties will appear to be done on the outside while still a bit mushy on the inside, so fry them a few minutes longer than you think they need.

PER SERVING

Calories: 202 — Fat: 9g — Sodium: 560mg — Fiber: 6g

Carbohydrates: 24g — Sugar: 0g — Protein: 6g

CHICKPEA SOFT TACOS
SERVES 4

Searching for more sources of plant-based protein? Look no further. Chickpeas, also known as garbanzo beans, are loaded with folate, zinc, protein, and dietary fiber—and they taste great! Toss these tasty morsels in meals throughout the week.

INGREDIENTS

2 cups (1½ cans) chickpeas, drained and rinsed

½ cup water

1 (6-ounce) can tomato paste

1 tablespoon chili powder

1 teaspoon garlic powder

½ teaspoon onion powder

½ teaspoon ground cumin

¼ cup chopped fresh cilantro

4 (6") whole-wheat tortillas

½ cup chopped white onion

½ cup chopped tomato

½ cup shredded lettuce

1. Combine chickpeas, water, tomato paste, chili powder, garlic powder, onion powder, and cumin in a large skillet. Cover and simmer over medium heat for 10 minutes, stirring occasionally. Uncover and simmer another 1–2 minutes or until most of the liquid is absorbed.

2. Use a fork or potato masher to mash the chickpeas until half mashed. Stir in fresh cilantro. Spoon the mixture into tortillas, add onion, tomato, and lettuce, and wrap.

PER SERVING
Calories: 289 – Fat: 5g – Sodium: 767mg – Fiber: 12g
Carbohydrates: 49g – Sugar: 11g – Protein: 12g

ORECCHIETTE WITH ROASTED PEPPERS, GREEN BEANS, AND PESTO

SERVES 8

Orecchiette are "little ears" of pasta—dime-sized concave disks that catch sauce very well and have a substantial, hearty bite. If you can't find them, look for conchiglie (small shells), which are similar.

INGREDIENTS

$1\frac{1}{2}$ tablespoons salt

8 ounces uncooked whole-wheat orecchiette

1 tablespoon olive oil, divided

2 teaspoons chopped fresh garlic

1 cup sliced roasted red pepper

$\frac{1}{4}$ pound green beans, blanched

$\frac{3}{4}$ cup store-bought pesto, divided

$\frac{1}{4}$ cup roughly chopped fresh Italian parsley

$\frac{1}{8}$ teaspoon salt

$\frac{1}{8}$ teaspoon ground black pepper

1 tablespoon unsalted butter

$\frac{1}{2}$ cup Parmesan cheese

6 lemon wedges

1. Add salt to a large pot of water and bring to a boil; cook pasta until al dente (still a little chewy). Drain pasta, but save 1 cup of the cooking water for later. In a large bowl, toss pasta with a drop of olive oil; set aside.

2. In a small bowl, combine olive oil and chopped garlic. Heat a large skillet 1 minute over medium heat. Add garlic oil; sizzle 15 seconds, then add roasted peppers and green beans. Sauté 3 minutes. Add $\frac{1}{2}$ cup pesto; stir.

3. Add cooked pasta, parsley, salt, pepper, and butter; simmer until heated through, adding a few drops of the reserved pasta water to make it saucy.

4. Remove from heat; toss with cheese. Serve with lemon wedges and the remaining pesto on the side.

PER SERVING

Calories: 263 – Fat: 14g – Sodium: 614mg – Fiber: 3g
Carbohydrates: 26g – Sugar: 3g – Protein: 7g

GARDEN QUESADILLAS
SERVES 4

As a college student, you have probably had your fair share of quesadillas. Try these Garden Quesadillas for a healthier plant-based version of this college staple. Add cilantro for an even fresher taste.

INGREDIENTS

2 tablespoons olive oil, divided

I medium yellow onion, peeled and chopped

I medium red bell pepper, seeded and chopped

$\frac{1}{2}$ cup chopped button mushrooms

I cup salsa

8 (6") whole-wheat tortillas

I cup fresh baby spinach leaves

I cup shredded pepper jack cheese

1. In medium skillet over medium heat, heat I table-spoon oil. Add onion and cook until crisp-tender, about 4 minutes. Add bell pepper and mushrooms and cook 2–4 minutes longer until tender. Drain vegetables and combine in medium bowl with salsa.

2. Arrange tortillas on a work surface. Top half of the tortillas with some of the baby spinach leaves and spoon the onion mixture on top. Top each with cheese, then remaining tortillas and press down gently.

3. Heat medium skillet over medium heat. Brush with remaining olive oil, then grill quesadillas, turning once and pressing down occasionally with spatula until cheese melts and tortillas are toasted. Cut into quarters and serve immediately.

PER SERVING
Calories: 409 – Fat: 17g – Sodium: 887mg – Fiber: 9g
Carbohydrates: 51g – Sugar: 12g – Protein: 14g

VEGAN STROGANOFF
SERVES 4

Another example of creative plant-based updating of a well-known recipe. Here the heavy cream that's traditionally used in a stroganoff dish is replaced with vegan yogurt thickened with ground flaxseed.

INGREDIENTS

1 tablespoon olive oil

2 (14-ounce) packages extra-firm tofu, crumbled

1 medium yellow onion, peeled and minced

1 cup sliced button mushrooms

1 teaspoon garlic powder

2 tablespoons soy sauce

1 (12-ounce) container cottage cheese

2 tablespoons plain soy yogurt

16 ounces whole-wheat noodles, cooked

2 teaspoons ground black pepper

1. Prepare a large skillet with olive oil over medium heat.

2. Sauté tofu crumbles and onion in the olive oil 7 minutes or until cooked through.

3. Add mushrooms, garlic powder, and soy sauce and combine well.

4. Stir in cottage cheese and soy yogurt until the ingredients become a thick sauce. Remove from the heat.

5. In a large bowl, combine cooked noodles, the tofu mixture, and pepper and blend well. Serve immediately.

PER SERVING
Calories: 491 – Fat: 18g – Sodium: 771mg – Fiber: 6g
Carbohydrates: 46g – Sugar: 6g – Protein: 38g

The Answer to Heavy Cream
Packed with fat and calories, heavily processed, and possibly containing hormones, antibiotics, and steroids, heavy dairy cream is a healthy-eating nightmare! In recipes that include this classic creamy recipe staple, try using plain Greek-style yogurt or vegan yogurt thickened with ground flaxseed for a perfect protein-packed substitute to the unhealthy alternative.

VEGGIE-STUFFED ZUCCHINI
SERVES 4

This recipe contains healthy and delicious plant-based protein. Stuff the zucchini with any vegetables you like. The vegetables in this recipe can easily be substituted with your favorites.

INGREDIENTS

4 medium zucchini

1 teaspoon salt

2 teaspoons vegan margarine

2 teaspoons vegetable oil

1 medium yellow onion, peeled and chopped

1 medium clove garlic, peeled and crushed

1/2 cup canned chickpeas, drained and rinsed

2 tablespoons all-purpose flour

1 teaspoon ground coriander

1 medium white potato, peeled, cooked, and diced

1 cup canned green peas, drained and rinsed

2 tablespoons chopped fresh cilantro

1. Preheat oven to 375°F.

2. Cut each zucchini in half lengthwise and scoop out the pulp. Place each half with the open side up in a shallow roasting pan and sprinkle with salt.

3. Heat margarine and oil in a large skillet over medium heat. Add onion and garlic; sauté for 4 minutes, then stir in chickpeas, flour, coriander, potato, peas, and cilantro.

4. Spoon one-quarter of the potato mixture into each zucchini half and cover with foil.

5. Bake for 15 minutes or until zucchini is tender.

PER SERVING

Calories: 179 — Fat: 4g — Sodium: 747mg — Fiber: 5g

Carbohydrates: 30g — Sugar: 7g — Protein: 7g

SPAGHETTI WITH SWEET CORN, TOMATOES, AND GOAT CHEESE

SERVES 4

Early fall at the beginning of the school year is the perfect time to scoop up sweet seasonal vegetables like scallions, corn, and tomatoes. When vegetables are ripe, they do all the work for you in a dish like this.

INGREDIENTS

8 ounces uncooked whole-wheat spaghetti

2 tablespoons unsalted butter

4 medium scallions, chopped

2 cups fresh corn kernels (about 3 ears)

1 cup diced red bell pepper

1 medium jalapeño pepper, seeded and finely chopped

3 medium tomatoes, diced

$1/4$ cup chopped fresh cilantro, plus 2 tablespoons for garnish, divided

$1/4$ cup water

$1/8$ teaspoon salt

$1/8$ teaspoon ground black pepper

2 ounces goat cheese, crumbled

1 large lemon, quartered

1. Cook pasta according to package directions.

2. Heat butter in a large skillet over medium heat. Add scallions, corn, red bell pepper, and jalapeño. Cook 3 minutes; add tomatoes, cilantro, and water. Season with salt and pepper.

3. Add the pasta. Sprinkle in crumbled cheese and toss to distribute. Divide into four portions and garnish with additional chopped cilantro and lemon wedges.

PER SERVING

Calories: 389 – Fat: 12g – Sodium: 140mg – Fiber: 11g
Carbohydrates: 62g – Sugar: 9g – Protein: 15g

"CHORIZO" RICE BOWL

SERVES 4

Typically, chorizo is a Spanish pork sausage made with smoked paprika and other spices, but this plant-based version is made with tofu instead. This "Chorizo" Rice Bowl is so delicious that you won't even miss the meat!

INGREDIENTS

RICE AND POTATO

1 cup uncooked brown rice

2½ cups Basic Vegetable Stock (see recipe in Chapter 8)

½ cup diced tomatoes

½ teaspoon salt

1 large sweet potato, peeled and diced

1 tablespoon olive oil

CHORIZO

8 ounces organic firm tofu

¼ cup finely chopped oil-packed sun-dried tomatoes

⅓ cup finely chopped button mushrooms

4 small cloves garlic, peeled and minced

¼ cup minced white onion

2 tablespoons apple cider vinegar

1½ tablespoons chili powder

½ teaspoon cayenne pepper

¾ teaspoon paprika

½ teaspoon ground cumin

⅛ teaspoon salt

¼ teaspoon ground black pepper

1 tablespoon olive oil

TO FINISH

1 medium ripe avocado, peeled, pitted, and sliced

1. **For Rice:** Add rice, Basic Vegetable Stock, tomatoes, and salt to a medium pot, and bring to a boil over medium-high heat. Reduce heat to medium, cover, and simmer 30 minutes or until Basic Vegetable Stock is absorbed.

2. **For Potato:** Preheat oven to 425°F. Line a 10" × 15" baking sheet with aluminum foil. Spread sweet potatoes evenly on the baking sheet and drizzle with olive oil. Bake 20 minutes or until potatoes just begin to crisp on the outside.

3. **For Chorizo:** Drain tofu and pat it dry with a paper towel. Add to a large bowl and mash with a fork until crumbled. Add sun-dried tomatoes, mushrooms, garlic, white onion, vinegar, chili powder, cayenne pepper, paprika, cumin, salt, and pepper. Toss until the mixture is evenly coated with the spices.

4. Heat oil in a large frying pan over medium heat. Add the chorizo mixture and cook 6–7 minutes, stirring occasionally, until slightly crispy.

5. **To finish:** Add rice to bowls, and top with sweet potato, chorizo, and avocado. Serve warm.

PER SERVING

Calories: 415 – Fat: 16g – Sodium: 507mg – Fiber: 8g

Carbohydrates: 58g – Sugar: 6g – Protein: 11g

SEITAN BUFFALO WINGS
SERVES 4

Perfect for serving at a college football watch party! If desired, you can cut some of the fat out of this recipe by skipping the breading and deep-frying. Instead, bake the seitan with the sauce for 25 minutes at 325°F.

INGREDIENTS

$1/3$ cup coconut oil

$1/3$ cup hot sauce

1 cup all-purpose flour

1 teaspoon garlic powder

1 teaspoon onion powder

$1/4$ teaspoon ground black pepper

$1/2$ cup soy milk

4 tablespoons vegetable oil

1 (16-ounce) package seitan

1. In a small saucepan over low heat, combine coconut oil and hot sauce just until oil is melted. Set aside.

2. In a small bowl, combine flour, garlic powder, onion powder, and pepper. Place soy milk in a separate small bowl. Heat oil in a medium skillet or stockpot over medium heat.

3. Dip each piece of seitan in the soy milk, then dredge in the flour mixture. Carefully place in hot oil and fry until lightly golden brown on all sides, about 4–5 minutes. Brush fried seitan with the coconut oil and hot sauce mixture. Serve.

PER SERVING
Calories: 465 — Fat: 31g — Sodium: 956mg — Fiber: 2g
Carbohydrates: 16g — Sugar: 1g — Protein: 22g

BARBECUE TEMPEH PIZZA
SERVES 2

This recipe gives you the flavors and tastes of the traditional version without packing your dish full of meat. Opt for whole-wheat pizza dough for even more plant-based protein. Make this dish instead of settling for dining hall pizza!

INGREDIENTS

1 pound whole-wheat pizza dough

8 ounces organic tempeh

$\frac{1}{4}$ cup plus 2 tablespoons barbecue sauce, divided

1 tablespoon olive oil, divided

1 cup shredded whole-milk mozzarella cheese

$\frac{1}{4}$ cup chopped white onion

1 tablespoon chopped fresh cilantro

1. Let dough rest on a floured surface for 30 minutes.

2. While dough is resting, crumble tempeh with your fingers and add to a medium bowl. Add $\frac{1}{4}$ cup barbecue sauce, and toss the tempeh until it's evenly coated.

3. Spread dough into a 12" circle, either stretching by hand or using a rolling pin. Lightly oil a large baking sheet, pizza pan, or pizza stone with $\frac{1}{2}$ tablespoon olive oil and place dough on top.

4. Brush the top of the pizza dough with remaining olive oil. Spread on remaining 2 tablespoons barbecue sauce, leaving space for the crust on the edges. Top with cheese, tempeh, and onion. Bake 8–10 minutes or until cheese is bubbly and crust is golden. Remove from oven, top with cilantro, and serve warm.

PER SERVING
Calories: 1,081 – Fat: 36g – Sodium: 2,056mg – Fiber: 17g
Carbohydrates: 135g – Sugar: 27g – Protein: 62g

EDAMAME PAD THAI
SERVES 2

Let's face it: As delicious as it is, pad thai isn't the healthiest of dinners. You also don't get much protein if you opt for a vegetarian version. However, with the few swaps made in this recipe, you can have a better-for-you plant-based meal with a balanced amount of nutrients.

INGREDIENTS

PAD THAI SAUCE

2 tablespoons soy sauce

1 tablespoon creamy peanut butter

1 tablespoon lime juice

1 tablespoon rice vinegar

1/2 tablespoon coconut sugar

1/4 teaspoon red pepper flakes

PAD THAI

1 tablespoon sesame oil

1 medium red bell pepper, seeded and thinly sliced

1/2 cup shredded carrots

1 cup cooked organic shelled edamame

4 ounces cooked brown rice pad thai noodles

TO FINISH

2 small green onions, finely chopped

3 sprigs fresh cilantro

1 teaspoon sesame seeds

1. **For Pad Thai Sauce:** Create sauce by mixing together ingredients in a small bowl until smooth.

2. **For Pad Thai:** In a large skillet, heat sesame oil over medium heat. Add bell pepper and carrots, and cook 2–3 minutes.

3. Add edamame, noodles, and sauce to the skillet and toss over low heat until well mixed and heated through, about 2 minutes.

4. **To finish:** Top with green onion, cilantro, and sesame seeds. Serve warm.

PER SERVING

Calories: 486 – Fat: 17g – Sodium: 931mg – Fiber: 11g
Carbohydrates: 66g – Sugar: 10g – Protein: 19g

Pad Thai Swaps
Feel like cutting down on carbs and adding in some vegetables? Consider making this Edamame Pad Thai with spiralized zucchini or sweet potato instead of the noodles. You can also toss in some cubed tofu for extra protein.

CHAPTER 7

DESSERTS AND DRINKS

No-Bake Cocoa Balls......................176

White Bean Blondies......................177

Chocolate Chip Cookies....................178

Chocolate Mocha Ice Cream............180

Chickpea Cookie Dough..................181

Foolproof Vegan Fudge...................182

Pumpkin Seed Bark.........................183

Peanut Butter Cups...........................185

Chocolate Tofu Pudding...................186

Easy Banana Date Cookies.............187

Sticky Dark Chocolate
Pistachio Bars....................................188

Black Bean Brownies.......................189

Banana Bread...................................190

Triple Chocolate Cupcakes...............191

Vegan Mango Ginger Ice.................192

Cocoa-Nut-Coconut
No-Bake Cookies..............................193

Banana Pineapple Yogurt Frosty....194

Red Bean Ice Cream Shake............196

Strawberry Protein Smoothie.........197

Green Smoothie Bowl......................198

Creamy Carrot Smoothie.................199

Blackberry Apple Smoothie............200

Green Bloody Mary..........................200

Matcha Smoothie.............................201

Sweet Potato Smoothie...................202

Salted Caramel Smoothie................203

NO-BAKE COCOA BALLS
SERVES 6

If you're someone who likes just a bite of dessert, you'll love these No-Bake Cocoa Balls. Eat as a dessert, for a quick boost of energy between classes, or as a late-night snack while doing homework.

INGREDIENTS

1 cup chopped pitted dates

1 cup raw cashews

$\frac{1}{4}$ cup unsweetened cocoa powder

1 tablespoon creamy peanut butter

$\frac{1}{4}$ cup sweetened coconut flakes

1. Cover dates in water and soak for about 10 minutes until softened. Drain.

2. Process dates, cashews, cocoa powder, and peanut butter in a food processor until combined and sticky. Add coconut flakes and process until coarse.

3. Shape into balls and chill. If the mixture is too wet, add more nuts and coconut, or add just a touch of water if the mixture is dry and crumbly.

PER SERVING
Calories: 240 — Fat: 12g — Sodium: 13mg — Fiber: 5g
Carbohydrates: 30g — Sugar: 18g — Protein: 7g

WHITE BEAN BLONDIES
MAKES 9 BLONDIES

Just like you can use black beans to make brownies in the Black Bean Brownies recipe later in this chapter, you can use white beans to make blondies here. But these blondies are so delicious that you would never know they're made primarily of beans. Surprise your roommates with this unique treat!

INGREDIENTS

1 1/2 cups canned cannellini beans, drained and rinsed

1/4 cup creamy peanut butter

2 tablespoons melted coconut oil

1 tablespoon vanilla extract

1/2 cup oat flour (rolled oats ground into flour)

1 cup coconut sugar

1/2 teaspoon baking powder

1/2 teaspoon salt

1/2 cup dark chocolate chips

1. Preheat oven to 350°F. Lightly grease an 8" × 8" baking dish with cooking spray.

2. In a blender or food processor, blend together white beans, peanut butter, coconut oil, and vanilla on high speed until the mixture is smooth, about 20–30 seconds. Transfer to a large bowl.

3. In a small bowl, combine oat flour, coconut sugar, baking powder, and salt. Add the dry mixture to the wet mixture and mix together evenly. Then mix in the chocolate chips.

4. Pour the batter into the baking dish, and bake 20–30 minutes until the tops of the blondies are golden and start to crack. Let cool before slicing.

PER SERVING (1 BLONDIE)
Calories: 275 – Fat: 12g – Sodium: 222mg – Fiber: 4g
Carbohydrates: 39g – Sugar: 27g – Protein: 5g

CHOCOLATE CHIP COOKIES
MAKES 24 COOKIES

This classic and delicious cookie is a perfect reward for studying. To make the recipe vegan, simply swap out the butter, eggs, and chocolate chips for their vegan counterparts!

INGREDIENTS

$2\frac{1}{2}$ cups all-purpose flour

1 teaspoon baking soda

1 teaspoon salt

1 cup (2 sticks) unsalted butter, softened

$\frac{3}{4}$ cup granulated sugar

$\frac{3}{4}$ cup packed light brown sugar

1 teaspoon vanilla extract

2 large eggs

2 cups semisweet chocolate chips

1. Preheat oven to 375°F.

2. In a medium bowl, whisk together flour, baking soda, and salt.

3. In a large bowl, cream together butter, granulated sugar, brown sugar, and vanilla extract.

4. Add the eggs one at a time to the sugar mixture, mixing until incorporated before adding the next one.

5. Add the flour mixture in three additions, mixing just enough to incorporate after each addition. Stir in the chocolate chips.

6. Drop the dough in tablespoon-sized scoops onto large ungreased baking sheets. Bake until golden, about 10 minutes.

7. Cool the pans a few minutes before transferring the cookies to a wire rack to cool completely.

PER SERVING (1 COOKIE)
Calories: 244 – Fat: 12g – Sodium: 160mg – Fiber: 1g
Carbohydrates: 33g – Sugar: 21g – Protein: 3g

CHOCOLATE MOCHA ICE CREAM
SERVES 6

Coffee lovers, this nondairy ice cream is for you. Reward yourself halfway through your late-night study session and get the energy boost you need to keep going with this Chocolate Mocha Ice Cream.

INGREDIENTS

1 cup vegan chocolate chips

1 cup soy milk

1 (12-ounce) block silken tofu

1/3 cup sugar

2 tablespoons instant coffee crystals

2 teaspoons vanilla extract

1/4 teaspoon salt

1. Using a double boiler, or over very low heat in a small saucepan, melt chocolate chips until smooth and creamy. Allow to cool slightly.

2. Combine soy milk, tofu, sugar, instant coffee, vanilla, and salt in a blender and blend until very smooth and creamy, at least 2 minutes. Add melted chocolate chips, and process until smooth.

3. Transfer the mixture to a large freezer-proof baking or casserole dish and freeze.

4. Stir every 30 minutes until a smooth ice cream forms, about 4 hours. If the mixture gets too firm, transfer to a blender and process until smooth, then return to freezer.

PER SERVING
Calories: 312 — Fat: 15g — Sodium: 132mg — Fiber: 3g
Carbohydrates: 35g — Sugar: 28g — Protein: 6g

CHICKPEA COOKIE DOUGH
SERVES 6

Eating cookie dough out of the bowl is definitely a guilty pleasure, but it's not exactly the healthiest choice. But with this Chickpea Cookie Dough, you can grab a spoon and eat this up without any regrets! You'll never believe it, but this cookie dough is made with just chickpeas and peanut butter—no butter, eggs, or sugar needed—so nibble on it guilt-free.

INGREDIENTS

1 (15-ounce) can chickpeas, drained and rinsed

$\frac{1}{2}$ cup creamy peanut butter

1 tablespoon maple syrup

$\frac{1}{2}$ teaspoon vanilla extract

$\frac{1}{8}$ teaspoon salt

$\frac{3}{4}$ cup dark chocolate chips

Combine chickpeas, peanut butter, maple syrup, vanilla, and salt in a blender or food processor and blend on high until smooth, about 20–30 seconds. Add to a large bowl, and mix in chocolate chips. Keep refrigerated up to three days.

PER SERVING
Calories: 361 – Fat: 22g – Sodium: 138mg – Fiber: 6g
Carbohydrates: 31g – Sugar: 16g – Protein: 9g

Don't Try to Make These Into Cookies
As delicious as this Chickpea Cookie Dough tastes, it unfortunately can't be baked into cookies, as this recipe is formulated to just be enjoyed "raw." If you try to bake this dough, you'll see that it won't expand or rise the way you want it to.

FOOLPROOF VEGAN FUDGE
MAKES 21 (1") PIECES

Let's be honest: No matter how you slice it, fudge is delicious. If you're a fan of nutty fudge, feel free to use crunchy peanut butter, or add in nuts as you see fit. Treat yourself to this Foolproof Vegan Fudge after a long day of classes.

INGREDIENTS

$\frac{1}{3}$ cup vegan margarine

$\frac{1}{3}$ cup unsweetened cocoa powder

$\frac{1}{3}$ cup soy cream

$\frac{1}{2}$ teaspoon vanilla extract

2 tablespoons creamy peanut butter

$3\frac{1}{2}$ cups powdered sugar

$\frac{3}{4}$ cup finely chopped walnuts

1. Lightly grease a small baking dish or square cake pan.

2. Using a double boiler, or over very low heat in a small saucepan, melt vegan margarine with cocoa, soy cream, vanilla, and peanut butter.

3. Slowly incorporate powdered sugar until the mixture is smooth, creamy, and thick. Stir in nuts.

4. Immediately transfer to pan and chill until completely firm, at least 2 hours.

PER SERVING (1 PIECE)
Calories: 120 – Fat: 5g – Sodium: 23mg – Fiber: 1g
Carbohydrates: 19g – Sugar: 17g – Protein: 1g

PUMPKIN SEED BARK
SERVES 8

Bark is an easy dessert that anyone can make, no matter your baking skills. For this fall-inspired dish, you need some quality dark chocolate to melt, some raw pumpkin seeds, and sea salt, and you have a sweet and salty treat that also doubles as a nice afternoon snack. Close your eyes when you eat it and you can practically feel the crisp autumn air!

INGREDIENTS

$\frac{1}{2}$ pound dark chocolate (70% or higher cocoa)

$\frac{1}{2}$ cup raw pumpkin seeds

$\frac{1}{4}$ teaspoon sea salt

1. Break chocolate into chunks. Melt chocolate by putting the chunks in a microwave-safe bowl and microwaving on high in 30-second increments, stirring after each time so the chocolate doesn't burn. Repeat until chocolate is melted, about 2 minutes.

2. Stir pumpkin seeds into melted chocolate. Spread a 10" × 15" baking sheet with parchment paper, and pour the chocolate mixture onto the parchment paper in an even layer using a rubber spatula, about $\frac{1}{3}$" thick.

3. Top with sea salt, and then let cool to room temperature. Refrigerate to set about 1 hour. To serve, break into pieces. Store in an airtight container in the refrigerator.

PER SERVING
Calories: 229 – Fat: 17g – Sodium: 49mg – Fiber: 3g
Carbohydrates: 14g – Sugar: 8g – Protein: 5g

PEANUT BUTTER CUPS
SERVES 8

A baked version of a popular candy, these biscuits make a delicious dessert. Skip the campus candy store and make your own! Use muffin tins with a 3½" diameter.

INGREDIENTS

½ cup crunchy peanut butter

1 (8-ounce) package soy cream cheese, at room temperature

¾ cup packed brown sugar

1 large egg, lightly beaten

3 tablespoons cornstarch

½ cup chocolate morsels

1 (16.3-ounce) tube flaky refrigerator biscuits

1. Preheat oven to 375°F. Spray muffin tins with non-stick cooking spray.

2. In a medium bowl, combine peanut butter, cream cheese, and brown sugar and beat until smooth.

3. Add egg and cornstarch and beat again. Fold the chocolate morsels in with a rubber spatula.

4. Roll out the biscuits one at a time on a lightly floured surface and fit each into a muffin cup so that it forms a "crust."

5. Spoon the peanut butter mixture into each biscuit crust. Reduce the oven temperature to 350°F.

6. Bake the cups 25–30 minutes or until the center feels firm to the touch. Remove from the oven and cool to firm completely.

PER SERVING

Calories: 520 – Fat: 25g – Sodium: 814mg – Fiber: 4g
Carbohydrates: 67g – Sugar: 32g – Protein: 10g

CHOCOLATE TOFU PUDDING
SERVES 4

This easy-to-make pudding tastes like an extravagantly decadent mousse with loads of cream, but its rich texture—and extra plant-based protein—comes from tofu. Be sure to use the "cook-and-serve" pudding, not the instant type.

INGREDIENTS

2 cups whole milk

1½ cups silken tofu

2 (1.3-ounce) boxes chocolate pudding mixture

1 cup chocolate morsels

1. Combine the milk, tofu, and pudding mixture in a blender and process until smooth. Pour the mixture into a medium saucepan. Heat slowly over medium-low heat, stirring constantly, until the mixture thickens.

2. Remove from heat, stir in chocolate morsels, and pour into a heatproof bowl. Chill until ready to serve.

PER SERVING

Calories: 417 – Fat: 19g – Sodium: 179mg – Fiber: 4g
Carbohydrates: 54g – Sugar: 40g – Protein: 13g

EASY BANANA DATE COOKIES
SERVES 12

Dates can easily satisfy a sweet tooth. These cookies are simple and free of refined sugar. Even though they're healthy, be sure to practice portion control because coconut flakes are nonetheless a high-fat food.

INGREDIENTS

1 cup chopped pitted dates

1 medium ripe banana, peeled

1/4 teaspoon vanilla extract

1 3/4 cups unsweetened coconut flakes

1. Preheat oven to 375°F. Cover dates in water and soak for about 10 minutes until softened. Drain.

2. Process together dates, banana, and vanilla in a food processor until almost smooth. Stir in coconut flakes with a rubber spatula until thick. You may need a little more or less than 1 3/4 cups.

3. Drop by generous tablespoonfuls onto a greased cookie sheet. Bake 10–12 minutes or until done. Cookies will be soft and chewy.

PER SERVING
Calories: 129 – Fat: 8g – Sodium: 2mg – Fiber: 3g
Carbohydrates: 15g – Sugar: 9g – Protein: 1g

STICKY DARK CHOCOLATE PISTACHIO BARS

MAKES 9 BARS

These pistachio bars are filled with all the goods, including nuts, seeds, and oats, making them a healthy powerhouse. These decadent bars are meant to be sticky, but the longer you refrigerate them, the firmer they'll get.

INGREDIENTS

1 cup pitted Medjool dates

2 tablespoons creamy almond butter

1 tablespoon tahini

1 tablespoon unsweetened cocoa powder

$\frac{1}{4}$ cup maple syrup

$\frac{1}{2}$ cup rolled oats

2 tablespoons chia seeds

2 tablespoons hemp seeds

$\frac{1}{2}$ cup pistachio meats, plus 1 teaspoon crushed pistachios

$\frac{1}{2}$ cup chopped dark chocolate (70% or higher cocoa)

1. Blend together dates, almond butter, tahini, cocoa powder, and maple syrup in a food processor or blender on high speed until a smooth paste forms, about 1–2 minutes. Transfer to a large bowl.

2. Mix in oats, chia seeds, hemp seeds, and pistachios. Line an 8" × 8" baking dish with parchment paper, and spread the mixture evenly into the dish. Press down flat with a spatula or the back of a spoon.

3. Add dark chocolate to a medium microwave-safe bowl. Microwave on high in 30-second increments until melted (about 1–2 minutes total depending on your microwave's wattage).

4. Drizzle the chocolate over the bars. Refrigerate 3–4 hours to set. Cut into squares. Keep refrigerated up to a week.

PER SERVING (1 BAR)
Calories: 232 – Fat: 11g – Sodium: 3mg – Fiber: 5g
Carbohydrates: 29g – Sugar: 18g – Protein: 6g

BLACK BEAN BROWNIES
MAKES 12 BROWNIES

You'll be so surprised by the way this fudgy dessert tastes that you won't even realize that it contains beans. The black beans blend together with the cocoa powder and coconut sugar to create a chocolatey brownie that's both vegan and gluten-free (as long as you get dairy-free chocolate chips). Make these for the next college bake sale; they're guaranteed to be a hit!

INGREDIENTS

$\frac{1}{4}$ cup plus 1 teaspoon melted coconut oil, divided

3 tablespoons warm water

2 tablespoons flaxseed meal

1 (15-ounce) can unsalted black beans, drained and rinsed

$\frac{1}{4}$ cup almond flour

$\frac{1}{4}$ cup unsweetened cocoa powder

$\frac{1}{2}$ cup coconut sugar

1 teaspoon vanilla extract

$\frac{1}{4}$ teaspoon salt

1 teaspoon baking powder

$\frac{1}{4}$ cup semisweet chocolate chips

1. Preheat oven to 350°F. Grease an 8" × 8" baking dish with 1 teaspoon coconut oil. Prepare the flaxseed "egg" by adding water and flaxseed to a small bowl. Stir and let sit for 15 minutes until flaxseeds are gummy.

2. Add all the ingredients, except the chocolate chips, to a blender or food processor, and blend on high speed until the mixture is smooth, about a minute or so.

3. Spoon the batter evenly into the baking dish. Bake 20–30 minutes until the outside begins to get crisp. Let cool 15 minutes to set. Brownies will be chewy but will become firmer as they set. Store in the refrigerator to keep longer.

PER SERVING (1 BROWNIE)
Calories: 147 – Fat: 7g – Sodium: 44mg – Fiber: 3g
Carbohydrates: 19g – Sugar: 10g – Protein: 3g

Salt in Black Beans
To avoid making these brownies unnecessarily salty, be sure to buy low- or no-sodium black beans. Or, make your own using dried beans at home, and just don't add salt.

BANANA BREAD
SERVES 8

This updated Banana Bread recipe is vegan and gluten-free. Be sure to use ripe bananas when making this dish: They'll ensure a moist bread and add a sweeter flavor than green or yellow bananas. You can make variations of this Banana Bread by mixing in other ingredients in addition to the walnuts; try dried fruit, chocolate chips, and other types of nuts or seeds.

INGREDIENTS

3 medium ripe peeled bananas, plus
   I peeled and sliced banana for topping

$1/4$ cup melted coconut oil

$1/4$ cup unsweetened almond milk

I teaspoon vanilla extract

$1 1/2$ cups almond flour

$1/2$ cup DIY Protein Powder
   (see recipe in Chapter 8)

$1/2$ cup coconut sugar

I teaspoon ground cinnamon

$1/2$ teaspoon baking soda

I teaspoon baking powder

$1/2$ teaspoon salt

$1/4$ cup chopped walnuts

1. Preheat oven to 350°F. Spray a 9" × 5" loaf pan with nonstick spray.

2. In a large bowl, mash three bananas with a fork, leaving them a little bit chunky. Add coconut oil, almond milk, and vanilla, and stir until combined.

3. In a medium bowl, combine almond flour, DIY Protein Powder, coconut sugar, cinnamon, baking soda, baking powder, and salt. Fold the dry mixture into the wet mixture until evenly combined. Then fold in walnuts.

4. Transfer the batter to the pan and top with remaining sliced banana. Bake 45 minutes to I hour until top is firm and comes out mostly clean with a toothpick. Let cool before cutting into slices.

PER SERVING
Calories: 382 – Fat: 25g – Sodium: 291mg – Fiber: 7g
Carbohydrates: 34g – Sugar: 20g – Protein: 9g

TRIPLE CHOCOLATE CUPCAKES
MAKES 16 CUPCAKES

Your reward for acing that test! A cross between a brownie and a muffin, these elegant treats have an intense chocolate flavor heightened by the cocoa powder.

INGREDIENTS

4 ounces unsweetened chocolate squares

$\frac{1}{2}$ pound (2 sticks) unsalted butter

6 large eggs

1 cup sugar

$\frac{3}{4}$ cup cake flour

1$\frac{1}{2}$ teaspoons baking powder

2 teaspoons vanilla extract

1 tablespoon unsweetened cocoa powder

$\frac{1}{8}$ teaspoon salt

1 cup mini chocolate morsels

1. Preheat oven to 350°F. Spray nonstick muffin cups with nonstick cooking spray.

2. In a small saucepan, melt chocolate and butter together over low heat. When melted, cool to room temperature.

3. Meanwhile, in a large bowl, beat the eggs with the sugar until the mixture turns a pale lemon-yellow. Spoon the cooled chocolate mixture into the sugar mixture and stir until combined. Stir in the cake flour, baking powder, vanilla, cocoa powder, and salt and beat about 30 seconds. Stir in the chocolate morsels.

4. Spoon the mixture into the muffin cups until each is about two-thirds full.

5. Bake 15–18 minutes or until a toothpick inserted in the center comes out clean and the cupcakes feel firm. Cool completely.

PER SERVING (1 CUPCAKE)
Calories: 304 – Fat: 19g – Sodium: 102mg – Fiber: 2g
Carbohydrates: 26g – Sugar: 18g – Protein: 5g

VEGAN MANGO GINGER ICE
SERVES 6

Select ripe mangoes, preferably the flat yellow varieties available seasonally. These have a subtle, sweet flavor that works well with fresh ginger. For fun, make ice pops: You can find molds at a home-goods store or online.

INGREDIENTS

3 cups water

2 cups sugar

6 tablespoons fresh lime juice

1 tablespoon grated fresh ginger

3 large ripe mangoes, peeled, pitted, and sliced

1 teaspoon fresh lime zest

1. Combine water and sugar in a large saucepan and cook over medium-low heat until the sugar dissolves entirely and the mixture turns slightly syrupy.

2. Combine sugar syrup and remaining ingredients in the container of a blender and process until smooth. Scoop the mixture into a container and freeze.

PER SERVING
Calories: 363 — Fat: 1g — Sodium: 2mg — Fiber: 3g
Carbohydrates: 93g — Sugar: 90g — Protein: 1g

COCOA-NUT-COCONUT NO-BAKE COOKIES
MAKES 24 COOKIES

Instead of settling for the bland processed-flour cookies from the dining hall, why not get some nutrients out of your dessert with these Cocoa-Nut-Coconut No-Bake Cookies? Not only do they require just a few ingredients, but they're also dairy-free and vegan!

INGREDIENTS

$\frac{1}{4}$ cup vegan margarine

$\frac{1}{2}$ cup soy milk

2 cups sugar

$\frac{1}{3}$ cup unsweetened cocoa powder

$\frac{1}{2}$ cup creamy peanut butter

$\frac{1}{2}$ teaspoon vanilla extract

3 cups quick-cooking oats

$\frac{1}{2}$ cup finely chopped walnuts

$\frac{1}{2}$ cup unsweetened coconut flakes

1. Line a large baking sheet with wax paper.

2. In a large saucepan over medium heat, melt vegan margarine and soy milk together and add sugar and cocoa. Bring to a quick boil to dissolve sugar, then reduce heat to low and stir in peanut butter, just until melted.

3. Remove from heat and stir in remaining ingredients. Allow to cool slightly.

4. Spoon about 3 tablespoons of the mixture at a time onto wax paper and press lightly to form a cookie shape. Chill until firm.

PER SERVING (1 COOKIE)
Calories: 172 – Fat: 6g – Sodium: 21mg – Fiber: 2g
Carbohydrates: 26g – Sugar: 18g – Protein: 3g

BANANA PINEAPPLE YOGURT FROSTY

SERVES 2

When you're dreaming of summer vacation, use this Banana Pineapple Yogurt Frosty to transport you away to a tropical beach. For a winning taste, look for a fruit yogurt made from a combination of fruits.

INGREDIENTS

1½ cups soy milk

1 (6-ounce) container tropical fruit yogurt

2 medium ripe bananas, peeled

1 cup well-drained canned crushed pineapple

2 teaspoons vanilla extract

2 teaspoons sugar

⅛ teaspoon ground nutmeg

1. Combine all the ingredients in a blender and process until smooth.

2. Pour the mixture into a suitable freezer container and chill in the freezer about 30 minutes or until ice forms around the edges of the container. Stir again and serve.

PER SERVING
Calories: 336 — Fat: 4g — Sodium: 113mg — Fiber: 5g
Carbohydrates: 66g — Sugar: 50g — Protein: 10g

RED BEAN ICE CREAM SHAKE
SERVES 4

Your post-midterms reward! Red bean paste is a sweetened purée found in Asian groceries; it's an excellent plant-based source of both protein and fiber. The ice cream and milk in this recipe provide even more protein.

INGREDIENTS

1 pint vanilla ice cream

1 1/2 cups red bean paste

1 cup 2% milk

Combine everything in a blender and blend until smooth.

PER SERVING
Calories: 482 — Fat: 8g — Sodium: 129mg — Fiber: 4g
Carbohydrates: 91g — Sugar: 69g — Protein: 10g

Make Your Own
To make your own sweet red beans, which can be puréed in a blender or food processor to make red bean paste, soak 1 cup dried adzuki beans in water overnight. Drain and put the beans in a large saucepan with 4 cups water and simmer for 90 minutes over medium heat. Stir in 1/2 cup sugar and cook for 10 more minutes, stirring often. Squash the beans with a wooden spoon in the saucepan and stir to thicken. Remove from heat and purée in a blender or food processor for a smoother paste. Chill in the refrigerator before using.

STRAWBERRY PROTEIN SMOOTHIE
SERVES 2

If you're tempted by those rows of fancy-looking dairy- and egg-based protein powders at your campus gym, try a vegan version! Well-stocked natural-foods stores sell a variety of naturally vegan protein powders that you can add to a smoothie for all your muscle-building needs. Or try the DIY Protein Powder recipe in Chapter 8.

INGREDIENTS

½ cup frozen strawberries

½ (14-ounce) block silken tofu

1 medium banana, peeled

¾ cup orange juice

4 ice cubes

1 tablespoon honey

Blend together all ingredients in a blender until smooth and creamy.

PER SERVING
Calories: 202 — Fat: 3g — Sodium: 38mg — Fiber: 3g
Carbohydrates: 38g — Sugar: 37g — Protein: 8g

GREEN SMOOTHIE BOWL
SERVES 2

Incorporate all your nutrients without having to make separate dishes on busy school days with this Green Smoothie Bowl. This smoothie is thick and topped with a variety of delicious garnishes, so it's best eaten in a bowl, although it can be made into a regular smoothie as well using nonfrozen bananas. Add minced ginger for an extra kick.

INGREDIENTS

2 frozen medium bananas, peeled and sliced

1 cup fresh spinach leaves

$\frac{1}{4}$ cup pea protein powder

1 cup unsweetened almond milk

4 strawberries, thinly sliced with tops removed

5 blackberries

2 tablespoons chia seeds

1 tablespoon unsweetened shredded coconut

1. Add bananas, spinach, protein powder, and almond milk to a blender and blend on high speed until smooth, about 10–20 seconds.

2. Pour smoothie into a large bowl and top with strawberries, blackberries, chia seeds, and unsweetened coconut. Serve immediately.

PER SERVING
Calories: 338 – Fat: 8g – Sodium: 236mg – Fiber: 15g
Carbohydrates: 58g – Sugar: 30g – Protein: 17g

How to Make the Perfect Smoothie Bowl
To make a smoothie bowl that stays firm enough to put toppings on, you want to make sure the frozen banana is as cold as possible when you blend it. It's best to not take the banana out of the freezer until you're ready to put it into the blender.

CREAMY CARROT SMOOTHIE
SERVES 1

Yes, it sounds odd, but college is all about trying new things! The orange and lemon juices sweeten this smoothie, so you'll have all the benefits of carrot while still enjoying a tasty treat. Eating your vegetables doesn't get much easier than this.

INGREDIENTS

5 large carrots, peeled

1 tablespoon lemon juice

$\frac{1}{4}$ cup orange juice

$\frac{1}{2}$ cup nonfat plain yogurt

$\frac{1}{2}$ cup skim milk

1. Grate carrots in a blender or food processor. Separate the grated carrot from the juice using a fine strainer. Reserve the juice (you should have about $\frac{1}{4}$ cup).

2. Blend grated carrot, lemon juice, orange juice, yogurt, and milk until smooth, then blend in the carrot juice. Pour into a tall glass.

PER SERVING
Calories: 292 – Fat: 1g – Sodium: 408mg – Fiber: 10g
Carbohydrates: 58g – Sugar: 31g – Protein: 15g

The Low-Down on Carrots
Loaded with beta-carotene, which is essential for healthy eyes, skin, and cell respiration, carrots are a nutritious superfood that's cheap and available year-round. Always choose fresh carrots that are crisp and tight-skinned, not limp, marred, or covered in brown blemishes.

BLACKBERRY APPLE SMOOTHIE
SERVES 1

When berries are not in season, frozen berries will work just as well. Frozen berries can also add a nice texture to a berry smoothie. Test the texture as you blend to get the perfect fruity, crunchy blend.

INGREDIENTS

1 cup blackberries

1 medium apple, sliced

1 cup nonfat yogurt

$\frac{1}{2}$ cup skim milk

Combine all ingredients in a blender and process until smooth. Pour into a tall glass.

PER SERVING

Calories: 352 – Fat: 1g – Sodium: 249mg – Fiber: 13g
Carbohydrates: 69g – Sugar: 48g – Protein: 20g

GREEN BLOODY MARY
SERVES 2

This green version of the Bloody Mary has all the necessary ingredients to repair exactly what the alcoholic version destroys! You'll find that vegetable drinks such as this taste great and are very filling.

INGREDIENTS

1 cup chopped watercress

2 large tomatoes

2 medium stalks celery

$\frac{1}{2}$ large lemon, peeled

1 tablespoon horseradish

$\frac{1}{2}$ teaspoon cayenne pepper

1 cup water, divided

1. Place watercress, tomatoes, celery, lemon, horse-radish, cayenne, and $\frac{1}{2}$ cup water in a blender and blend until thoroughly combined.

2. Add remaining $\frac{1}{2}$ cup water while blending until desired texture is achieved.

PER SERVING

Calories: 52 – Fat: 0g – Sodium: 47mg – Fiber: 5g
Carbohydrates: 12g – Sugar: 6g – Protein: 2g

MATCHA SMOOTHIE
SERVES 1

Green tea is one of the healthiest beverages out there, and you can incorporate it into your smoothies by using matcha tea powder. This traditional Japanese drink is as rich in flavor as it is color, and blending it with the banana and cashews gives it some creaminess. The caffeine in the green tea will keep you alert throughout the day, and thanks to the spinach, cashews, and hemp seeds in this smoothie, you'll also get your fair share of antioxidants and protein.

INGREDIENTS

1 cup unsweetened almond milk

1 teaspoon matcha powder

1 large banana, peeled and sliced

1 cup fresh spinach leaves

2 tablespoons raw cashews

2 tablespoons hemp seeds

Add all ingredients to a blender and blend on high speed until smooth, about 10–20 seconds. Serve immediately.

PER SERVING

Calories: 373 — Fat: 20g — Sodium: 206mg — Fiber: 7g

Carbohydrates: 42g — Sugar: 18g — Protein: 14g

SWEET POTATO SMOOTHIE
SERVES 1

Most smoothies are made with a lot of fruit, and although that makes them taste delicious, it can also make them high in sugar. This smoothie is low in sugar because it doesn't contain any fruit—just sweet potato and a drizzle of maple syrup.

INGREDIENTS

1 medium sweet potato, peeled

2 tablespoons creamy almond butter

1 tablespoon chia seeds

1 cup unsweetened almond milk

$\frac{1}{2}$ teaspoon maple syrup

$\frac{1}{4}$ teaspoon ground cinnamon

5 ice cubes

1. Cook sweet potato by poking holes in it with a fork and microwaving 4–5 minutes or until soft. Let cool for a few minutes.

2. Add sweet potato along with all other ingredients to a blender and blend on high until smooth, about 10–20 seconds. Serve immediately.

PER SERVING

Calories: 386 – Fat: 22g – Sodium: 224mg – Fiber: 12g
Carbohydrates: 39g – Sugar: 11g – Protein: 12g

SALTED CARAMEL SMOOTHIE
SERVES 1

Ditch that Frappuccino and opt for a homemade Salted Caramel Smoothie instead. This drink doesn't contain any refined sugar, and it gets its decadent caramel taste from the rich Medjool dates. If you want the drink to be even richer and creamier, you can use 1 cup canned coconut milk instead of almond milk.

INGREDIENTS

- 1 large frozen banana, peeled and sliced

- 3 Medjool dates

- 1 cup unsweetened almond milk

- $\frac{1}{8}$ teaspoon salt

- $\frac{1}{4}$ cup DIY Protein Powder (see recipe in Chapter 8)

Add all ingredients to a blender and blend on high until smooth, about 10–20 seconds. Serve immediately.

PER SERVING

Calories: 638 – Fat: 24g – Sodium: 474mg – Fiber: 18g
Carbohydrates: 100g – Sugar: 65g – Protein: 17g

Benefits of Using Dates over Cane Sugar
Although it's plant-based and tastes good, cane sugar has absolutely no nutritional value. Dates, on the other hand, contain dietary fiber, antioxidants, and a number of vitamins and minerals.

CHAPTER 8

STAPLE RECIPES

Baked Tortilla Chips............................206

Fresh and Spicy Salsa 207

Basic Marinara....................................209

Kale Pesto 210

Raspberry Vinaigrette 211

Red Garlic Mayonnaise (Rouille)...212

Amish Apple Butter...........................213

Roasted Red Pepper Hummus......214

Basic Vegetable Stock 216

Mango Citrus Salsa 217

Basic Balsamic Vinaigrette 218

DIY Protein Powder..........................219

Vegan Chocolate Hazelnut Spread...221

Homemade Nut Milk 222

Easy Homemade Pizza Sauce.........223

Guacamole 224

Classic Hummus..................................226

Italian Dressing...................................227

Green and Black Olive Tapenade...228

BAKED TORTILLA CHIPS
SERVES 10

Instead of stocking up with bags of oily chips and crackers, keep corn tortillas in the refrigerator and bake up an exact amount of chips whenever the need arises. To make whole-wheat tortilla chips, simply choose whole-wheat tortillas.

INGREDIENTS

10 (6") corn tortillas

$\frac{1}{8}$ teaspoon salt

1. Preheat oven to 400°F. Cover two cookie sheets with nonstick spray. Cut each tortilla into six wedges. Scatter wedges onto cookie sheets.

2. Spray wedges with nonstick cooking spray and sprinkle with salt. Bake for 12 minutes.

PER SERVING
Calories: 52 – Fat: 1g – Sodium: 39mg – Fiber: 2g
Carbohydrates: 11g – Sugar: 0g – Protein: 2g

Try Different Varieties
You know how tortilla chips come in all kinds of flavors these days? So can your homemade chips! The trick is in selecting different kinds of tortillas. For example, try whole-wheat tortillas for a healthy option, or roasted red pepper tortillas for some extra color and flavor.

FRESH AND SPICY SALSA
MAKES 3 CUPS

Combining fresh and roasted tomatoes adds a great depth of flavor to this easy salsa recipe. Serve with your favorite whole-wheat or corn tortillas, in a burrito, on top of nachos, and more. To adjust for spice, add or take out the jalapeños as you see fit.

INGREDIENTS

3 pounds tomatoes

4 medium cloves garlic, peeled and minced

2 tablespoons olive oil

$\frac{1}{2}$ teaspoon salt

1 medium jalapeño pepper

1 green bell pepper, seeded and chopped

$\frac{1}{2}$ cup chopped red onion

2 tablespoons lemon juice

$\frac{1}{8}$ teaspoon cayenne pepper

1. Preheat oven to 400°F. Cut three tomatoes in half; place cut-side up on a cookie sheet. Top each tomato with some garlic. Drizzle with olive oil and sprinkle with salt. Roast for 15–25 minutes or until tomatoes have some brown spots. Remove from oven and cool.

2. Chop remaining tomatoes and place in a large bowl. Seed and mince jalapeño and add to chopped tomatoes along with green pepper and onion.

3. Chop cooled roasted tomatoes and add to salsa. Sprinkle with lemon juice and cayenne pepper and stir gently. Cover and chill for 1–2 hours before serving.

PER SERVING ($\frac{1}{4}$ CUP)
Calories: 45 – Fat: 2g – Sodium: 102mg – Fiber: 2g
Carbohydrates: 6g – Sugar: 3g – Protein: 1g

Salsa Is Simple
Why buy prepared salsa at the store when you can make your own from scratch? Making salsa at home allows you to save money and customize according to your tastes. In the mood for a hearty bean salsa? Throw in some black or pinto beans. Craving a fresher garden salsa? Add in some fresh corn. The possibilities are endless.

BASIC MARINARA
MAKES 1 QUART

August and September are tomato harvest season in the East, when thousands of cooks pack summer's bounty into jars of fruity tomato. Freeze or can this sauce at the beginning of the school year to last all semester. Serve over whole-wheat pasta or zoodles (zucchini noodles) as desired.

INGREDIENTS

4 pounds Roma tomatoes

2 tablespoons olive oil

1 large yellow onion, peeled and roughly chopped

5 medium cloves garlic, peeled and chopped

1 teaspoon sugar

2 tablespoons tomato paste

1/8 teaspoon salt

1/8 teaspoon ground black pepper

1 cup stemmed fresh basil leaves

1. Halve the tomatoes and squeeze out as many seeds as you can. Dice the tomatoes.

2. In a large saucepan or Dutch oven over medium heat, heat oil until hot enough to sizzle when a piece of onion is added. Add onions; cook until soft and beginning to brown slightly, about 10 minutes.

3. Stir in garlic, sugar, and tomato paste and cook 2 minutes more, stirring constantly. Add the tomatoes and cook 10 minutes until the mixture becomes frothy.

4. Lower heat to a slow simmer and cook 30 minutes more until all tomatoes are fully softened; season with salt and pepper. If you prefer chunky sauce, add basil and serve. For smooth sauce, transfer the mixture to a blender, purée, and strain, then add the basil leaves at the end.

PER SERVING (1/3 CUP)
Calories: 53 – Fat: 2g – Sodium: 52mg – Fiber: 2g
Carbohydrates: 8g – Sugar: 5g – Protein: 2g

KALE PESTO

MAKES 2½ CUPS

Kale's cholesterol-reducing properties are actually stronger if it's steamed. Steaming reduces the leafy green's strong taste and helps it retain its bright color. The final product freezes well; freeze in small portions for up to several months and thaw in the refrigerator overnight before using.

INGREDIENTS

2 cups packed chopped fresh kale

1 cup fresh basil leaves

½ cup toasted chopped hazelnuts

1 tablespoon lemon juice

1 medium clove garlic, peeled and minced

½ teaspoon salt

⅛ teaspoon ground black pepper

⅓ cup olive oil

2 tablespoons hazelnut oil

¼ cup water

1. Bring 2 cups water to a boil in a medium saucepan. Place kale in a steamer basket and put it in the pan. Cover. Steam kale for 2–3 minutes or until slightly softened. Remove to a colander to drain. Press in kitchen towel to remove excess water.

2. Combine kale, basil, hazelnuts, lemon juice, garlic, salt, and pepper in a food processor. Process until finely chopped.

3. With motor running, add olive oil and hazelnut oil gradually through the feed tube. Add water as needed for desired consistency. Store, covered, in the refrigerator for up to a week or freeze for longer storage.

PER SERVING (2 TABLESPOONS)
Calories: 69 – Fat: 7g – Sodium: 0mg – Fiber: 0g
Carbohydrates: 1g – Sugar: 0g – Protein: 1g

RASPBERRY VINAIGRETTE

SERVES 10

Create a colorful and inviting salad with this lovely purple dressing. Dress up a plain fruit salad, or toss some cranberries, chicken, and baby spinach with this vinaigrette for a gourmet touch.

INGREDIENTS

1/4 cup apple cider vinegar

2 tablespoons lime juice

1/4 cup raspberry purée

2 tablespoons Dijon mustard

1 tablespoon maple syrup

3/4 cup olive oil

1 teaspoon salt

1/2 teaspoon ground black pepper

1. Process together vinegar, lime juice, raspberry purée, mustard, and maple syrup in a food processor or blender until smooth.

2. Slowly add olive oil a few drops at a time on high speed to allow oil to emulsify. Season with salt and black pepper.

PER SERVING

Calories: 162 – Fat: 16g – Sodium: 308mg – Fiber: 1g
Carbohydrates: 3g   Sugar: 2g – Protein: 0g

RED GARLIC MAYONNAISE (ROUILLE)

MAKES 1½ CUPS

Roasted red peppers give this mayonnaise a smoky and delicious flavor. Use it as a spread for your sandwiches or as a dip to pack more plant-based protein into your meals and snacks.

INGREDIENTS

2 medium cloves garlic, peeled and chopped very fine

1 cup soy mayonnaise

1 small roasted red bell pepper, peeled and puréed

⅛ teaspoon salt

1 tablespoon fresh lemon juice

⅛ teaspoon cayenne pepper

In a medium bowl, whisk together garlic, mayonnaise, and roasted pepper purée. Season with salt, lemon juice, and cayenne.

PER SERVING (2 TABLESPOONS)
Calories: 38 – Fat: 3g – Sodium: 209mg – Fiber: 0g
Carbohydrates: 2g – Sugar: 1g – Protein: 2g

AMISH APPLE BUTTER

MAKES 8 CUPS

Traditionally flavored with warm spices, this condiment is called a "butter" due to its thick consistency and soft texture. Since apple butter needs a long, unhurried cooking period to caramelize the fruit and deepen the flavors, a slow cooker is the perfect place to make it.

INGREDIENTS

10 cups (about 5 pounds) peeled, cored, and quartered Gala apples

1 cup maple syrup

3 tablespoons lemon juice

1½ teaspoons ground cinnamon

½ teaspoon ground cloves

½ teaspoon allspice

1. Place apples in a 4-quart slow cooker greased with coconut oil.

2. Pour maple syrup and lemon juice over apples and add cinnamon, cloves, and allspice. Stir to coat apples.

3. Cover and cook on low for 14–16 hours until apple butter is a deep, dark brown and is richly flavored.

4. Ladle into clean, medium sterilized jars and store covered in the refrigerator for up to six weeks. You can also process and can the apple butter if you prefer.

PER SERVING (2 TABLESPOONS)
Calories: 21 — Fat: 0g — Sodium: 0mg — Fiber: 0g
Carbohydrates: 6g — Sugar: 5g — Protein: 0g

Old-Fashioned Apple Butter Making

Apple butter used to be made in large copper pots that simmered over a hot fire all day long. It was often done by a church group or by a large family who could share the responsibility of stirring the pot throughout the long day to keep the mixture from burning. Once finished, the apple butter would be canned and sold to raise money for a good cause or shared among all who helped make it.

ROASTED RED PEPPER HUMMUS
MAKES 1½ CUPS

As a vegetable dip or sandwich spread, hummus is always a favorite. Up the garlic in this recipe, if that's your thing, and don't be ashamed to lick the spoons or spatula.

INGREDIENTS

1 (15-ounce) can chickpeas, drained and rinsed

⅓ cup tahini

⅔ cup chopped roasted red peppers

3 tablespoons lemon juice

2 tablespoons olive oil

2 medium cloves garlic, peeled

½ teaspoon ground cumin

⅓ teaspoon salt

¼ teaspoon cayenne pepper

Process all ingredients together in a blender or food processor until smooth, scraping the sides down as needed.

PER SERVING (¼ CUP)
Calories: 182 – Fat: 11g – Sodium: 229mg – Fiber: 4g
Carbohydrates: 15g – Sugar: 3g – Protein: 6g

Do-It-Yourself Roasted Red Peppers

Sure, you can buy them in a jar, but it's easy to roast your own. Here's how: Fire up your oven to 450°F (or use the broiler setting) and drizzle a few whole peppers with olive oil. Bake 30 minutes, turning over once. Direct heat will also work, if you have a gas stove. Hold the peppers with tongs over the flame until lightly charred. Let your peppers cool, then remove the skin before making hummus.

BASIC VEGETABLE STOCK
SERVES 6

This versatile broth is much lower in sodium than the prepared varieties available in the supermarket. And it's high in disease-fighting phytonutrients. Try adding mushrooms for additional flavor.

INGREDIENTS

2 pounds yellow onions, peeled and roughly chopped

1 pound carrots, peeled and roughly chopped

1 pound celery, roughly chopped

$1\frac{1}{2}$ gallons water

1 cup chopped parsley stems

4 sprigs fresh thyme

2 bay leaves

15 peppercorns

1. Place onions, carrots, celery, and water in a large stockpot over medium heat; bring to a simmer and cook, uncovered, for $1\frac{1}{2}$ hours.

2. Add parsley stems, thyme, bay leaves, and peppercorns, and continue to simmer, uncovered, for 45 minutes.

3. Remove from heat and strain stock. Discard solids. Stock can be refrigerated for two to four days or frozen for up to three months.

PER SERVING

Calories: 21 — Fat: 0g — Sodium: 24mg — Fiber: 0g
Carbohydrates: 5g — Sugar: 2g — Protein: 0g

Homemade Stocks

Your homemade stocks give a special quality to all the dishes you use them in. Not only will the flavor of homemade stocks be better than that from purchased bases, but you will also have added your own personal touch to the meal. Always cook them uncovered, as covering will cause them to become cloudy.

MANGO CITRUS SALSA
SERVES 8

Salsa has a variety of uses, and this recipe adds color and variety to your usual chips and dip or Mexican dishes. Keep this stocked in the refrigerator for the perfect after-class snack.

INGREDIENTS

1 medium mango, chopped

2 medium tangerines, seeded and chopped

$\frac{1}{2}$ medium red bell pepper, seeded and chopped

$\frac{1}{2}$ medium red onion, peeled and minced

3 medium cloves garlic, peeled and minced

$\frac{1}{2}$ medium jalapeño pepper, seeded and minced

2 tablespoons lime juice

$\frac{1}{2}$ teaspoon salt

$\frac{1}{4}$ teaspoon ground black pepper

3 tablespoons chopped fresh cilantro

1. Gently toss together all ingredients.

2. Allow to sit for at least 15 minutes before serving to allow flavors to mingle.

PER SERVING
Calories: 56 — Fat: 0g — Sodium: 2mg — Fiber: 2g
Carbohydrates: 13g — Sugar: 10g — Protein: 1g

Hello, Mango
A ripe mango is sweet, with a unique taste that varies from variety to variety. The texture of the flesh varies as well, some have a soft, pulpy texture similar to an overripe plum, while others have firmer flesh like a cantaloupe or avocado. Mango lassi, or a mango smoothie, is a very popular choice in many Indian restaurants.

BASIC BALSAMIC VINAIGRETTE
MAKES 1 CUP

No need to purchase expensive and sugar-laden salad dressings at the grocery store anymore! Whip up this simple dressing in no time with ingredients you most likely already have on hand.

INGREDIENTS

$\frac{1}{4}$ cup balsamic vinegar

$\frac{1}{2}$ cup olive oil

1 tablespoon Dijon mustard

$\frac{1}{4}$ teaspoon salt

$\frac{1}{8}$ teaspoon ground black pepper

$\frac{1}{2}$ teaspoon dried basil

$\frac{1}{2}$ teaspoon dried parsley

Whisk together all ingredients with a fork until well combined.

PER SERVING (2 TABLESPOONS)
Calories: 130 — Fat: 13g — Sodium: 121mg — Fiber: 0g
Carbohydrates: 2g — Sugar: 1g — Protein: 0g

DIY PROTEIN POWDER
MAKES 2 CUPS

This protein powder recipe uses different types of seeds that are ground up and mixed together. You can find all these seeds at your regular grocery store. This DIY Protein Powder works best in heartier foods such as baked goods, soups, or sauces.

INGREDIENTS

¾ cup chia seeds

¾ cup raw unsalted sunflower seeds

¾ cup hemp seeds

¾ cup flaxseed meal

Grind together all ingredients in a food processor or blender on high speed until a fine powder has formed, about 10–20 seconds. Store in a lidded jar or other airtight container in a cool, dry place. DIY Protein Powder will keep for a few weeks.

PER SERVING (¼ CUP)
Calories: 288 – Fat: 21g – Sodium: 3mg – Fiber: 9g
Carbohydrates: 13g – Sugar: 0g – Protein: 13g

VEGAN CHOCOLATE HAZELNUT SPREAD

MAKES 1 CUP

You can use this spread on top of toast, as a dip for fruit, or you can give up after a late-night study session and eat it with a spoon. Garnish with chopped nuts and enjoy!

INGREDIENTS

2 cups chopped hazelnuts

$\frac{1}{2}$ cup unsweetened cocoa powder

$\frac{1}{2}$ cup powdered sugar

$\frac{1}{2}$ teaspoon vanilla extract

4 tablespoons vegetable oil

1. Add hazelnuts, cocoa powder, sugar, and vanilla to food processor and process to combine.

2. Add oil, just a little bit at a time, until the mixture is soft and creamy and desired consistency is reached. You may need to add a bit more or less than the 4 tablespoons.

PER SERVING (1 TABLESPOON)
Calories: 139 – Fat: 12g – Sodium: 0mg – Fiber: 2g
Carbohydrates: 7g – Sugar: 4g – Protein: 3g

HOMEMADE NUT MILK
SERVES 2

Homemade Nut Milk is delicious in breakfast cereal, oatmeal, smoothies, and more. If you don't have a sieve or cheesecloth, you can still enjoy this recipe, but it will be a bit grainy. Note that homemade nut milks aren't a good source of calcium; it's an added ingredient in store-bought versions.

INGREDIENTS

1 cup raw cashews

Water for soaking

Additional 4 cups water for milk

$\frac{1}{2}$ teaspoon salt

$\frac{1}{2}$ teaspoon vanilla extract

1. In a large bowl, cover nuts with plenty of water and allow to soak for at least 1 hour or overnight. Drain.

2. Blend soaked nuts with 4 cups water in a food processor or blender. Purée on high until smooth.

3. Strain through a cheesecloth or a sieve. Stir in salt and vanilla.

PER SERVING
Calories: 42 – Fat: 3g – Sodium: 581mg – Fiber: 0g
Carbohydrates: 4g – Sugar: 1g – Protein: 3g

EASY HOMEMADE PIZZA SAUCE
MAKES 1½ CUPS

Homemade pizza sauce is delicious. You'll welcome the switch from the campus pizza joint.

INGREDIENTS

1 tablespoon olive oil

½ cup chopped white onion

3 tablespoons tomato paste

1 cup tomato purée

1 tablespoon Dijon mustard

½ teaspoon salt

¼ teaspoon crushed red pepper flakes

1 teaspoon dried basil

1 teaspoon dried thyme

1 teaspoon dried oregano

¼ teaspoon ground black pepper

1. In a small saucepan over medium-low heat, combine olive oil and onion; cook and stir until tender, about 5 minutes.

2. Add all remaining ingredients and cook, stirring frequently, over low heat until thickened, about 15 minutes. Use as directed in a pizza recipe, or store, covered, in refrigerator up to five days.

PER SERVING (¼ CUP)

Calories: 58 – Fat: 3g – Sodium: 394mg – Fiber: 2g
Carbohydrates: 7g – Sugar: 4g – Protein: 2g

Canned Tomato Products

While the rule of thumb is to try to use fresh rather than canned vegetables in recipes, the rule bends a little in the case of tomatoes. Because tomato sauce needs a variety of ingredients in order to achieve the right flavor and consistency, you need a number of different items, such as tomato paste, crushed tomatoes, and tomato purée. Every recipe is different, but plan on visiting the canned tomato aisle in your grocery store when sauce is on the agenda.

GUACAMOLE
MAKES 3½ CUPS

While fresh guac might be rare in the dining hall, it doesn't have to be rare for you! Avocados are a unique fruit because they are naturally high in fat. Since you need some fat in your diet, the plant-based option provided by guacamole makes a really healthy choice. Serve with Baked Tortilla Chips (see recipe in this chapter).

INGREDIENTS

4 medium ripe avocados, peeled, pitted, and sliced

I small red onion, peeled and chopped

2 medium cloves garlic, peeled and finely chopped

3 tablespoons lemon juice

¼ cup salsa

1. Mash avocados in a medium bowl.

2. Mix onion, garlic, lemon juice, and salsa with the mashed avocado. Refrigerate briefly to give the flavors time to blend. Serve with tortilla chips for dipping.

PER SERVING (½ CUP)
Calories: 138 – Fat: 11g – Sodium: 72mg – Fiber: 6g
Carbohydrates: 9g – Sugar: 1g – Protein: 2g

CLASSIC HUMMUS
MAKES 2 CUPS

Feel free to experiment with different flavors by adding some sun-dried tomatoes, red pepper, or any of your favorite herbs for extra flavor. If you want a thinner hummus, add up to $\frac{1}{4}$ cup cold water to this recipe.

INGREDIENTS

2 large cloves garlic, peeled

1 (16-ounce) can chickpeas, drained and rinsed

3 tablespoons tahini

$\frac{1}{2}$ teaspoon coarse (kosher) salt

3 teaspoons toasted ground cumin

2 tablespoons fresh lemon juice, divided

$\frac{1}{4}$ cup plus 1 tablespoon olive oil, divided

$\frac{1}{8}$ teaspoon ground black pepper

$\frac{1}{8}$ teaspoon paprika

1 tablespoon chopped fresh parsley

1. In a food processor or blender, process garlic until it sticks to the sides of the bowl. Add chickpeas, tahini, salt, cumin, and half of the lemon juice. Process until smooth, gradually drizzling in the olive oil.

2. Season with pepper and remaining lemon juice, saving a few drops for garnish.

3. Spread onto plates and garnish with 1 tablespoon olive oil, lemon juice, paprika, and parsley.

PER SERVING ($\frac{1}{4}$ CUP)
Calories: 198 – Fat: 12g – Sodium: 285mg – Fiber: 5g
Carbohydrates: 17g – Sugar: 3g – Protein: 6g

ITALIAN DRESSING
SERVES 8

Try doubling this recipe and storing the dressing in a glass jar. It will keep for a week, and can be used for more recipes besides just salad! Experiment with sandwiches, pastas, spreads, stir-frys, and more!

INGREDIENTS

$\frac{1}{3}$ cup apple cider vinegar

$\frac{1}{2}$ teaspoon dry mustard

1 teaspoon lemon juice

2 medium cloves garlic, peeled and chopped

1 teaspoon dried oregano

$\frac{1}{2}$ teaspoon salt

$\frac{1}{2}$ teaspoon ground black pepper

$\frac{1}{2}$ cup olive oil

1. Place all ingredients except olive oil in a blender. With the blender running on a medium setting, slowly pour in oil. Blend until smooth.

2. Serve immediately on salad or cover and store in the refrigerator for up to seven days.

PER SERVING
Calories: 123 – Fat: 13g – Sodium: 146mg – Fiber: 0g
Carbohydrates: 1g – Sugar: 0g – Protein: 0g

GREEN AND BLACK OLIVE TAPENADE

MAKES 1 CUP

Mediterranean olive tapenade can be used as a spread or dip for slices of French bread or crackers—perfect for your next study party. If you don't have a food processor, you could also mash the ingredients together with a mortar and pestle or a large fork.

INGREDIENTS

$\frac{1}{2}$ cup green olives

$\frac{3}{4}$ cup black olives

2 medium cloves garlic, peeled

1 tablespoon capers

2 tablespoons lemon juice

2 tablespoons olive oil

$\frac{1}{4}$ teaspoon dried oregano

$\frac{1}{4}$ teaspoon ground black pepper

Process all ingredients in a food processor until almost smooth.

PER SERVING (1 TABLESPOON)

Calories: 39 – Fat: 4g – Sodium: 168mg – Fiber: 0g

Carbohydrates: 1g – Sugar: 0g – Protein: 0g

RESOURCES

US/METRIC CONVERSION CHART

VOLUME CONVERSIONS

US Volume Measure	Metric Equivalent
⅛ teaspoon	0.5 milliliter
¼ teaspoon	1 milliliter
½ teaspoon	2 milliliters
1 teaspoon	5 milliliters
½ tablespoon	7 milliliters
1 tablespoon (3 teaspoons)	15 milliliters
2 tablespoons (1 fluid ounce)	30 milliliters
¼ cup (4 tablespoons)	60 milliliters
⅓ cup	90 milliliters
½ cup (4 fluid ounces)	125 milliliters
⅔ cup	160 milliliters
¾ cup (6 fluid ounces)	180 milliliters
1 cup (16 tablespoons)	250 milliliters
1 pint (2 cups)	500 milliliters
1 quart (4 cups)	1 liter (about)

WEIGHT CONVERSIONS

US Weight Measure	Metric Equivalent
½ ounce	15 grams
1 ounce	30 grams
2 ounces	60 grams
3 ounces	85 grams
¼ pound (4 ounces)	115 grams
½ pound (8 ounces)	225 grams
¾ pound (12 ounces)	340 grams
1 pound (16 ounces)	454 grams

OVEN TEMPERATURE CONVERSIONS

Degrees Fahrenheit	Degrees Celsius
200 degrees F	95 degrees C
250 degrees F	120 degrees C
275 degrees F	135 degrees C
300 degrees F	150 degrees C
325 degrees F	160 degrees C
350 degrees F	180 degrees C
375 degrees F	190 degrees C
400 degrees F	205 degrees C
425 degrees F	220 degrees C
450 degrees F	230 degrees C

BAKING PAN SIZES

American	Metric
8 x 1½ inch round baking pan	20 x 4 cm cake tin
9 x 1½ inch round baking pan	23 x 3.5 cm cake tin
11 x 7 x 1½ inch baking pan	28 x 18 x 4 cm baking tin
13 x 9 x 2 inch baking pan	30 x 20 x 5 cm baking tin
2 quart rectangular baking dish	30 x 20 x 3 cm baking tin
15 x 10 x 2 inch baking pan	30 x 25 x 2 cm baking tin (Swiss roll tin)
9 inch pie plate	22 x 4 or 23 x 4 cm pie plate
7 or 8 inch springform pan	18 or 20 cm springform or loose bottom cake tin
9 x 5 x 3 inch loaf pan	23 x 13 x 7 cm or 2 lb narrow loaf or pâté tin
1½ quart casserole	1.5 liter casserole
2 quart casserole	2 liter casserole

APPENDIX
GLOSSARY OF BASIC COOKING TERMS

Al dente

A term used in Italian cooking that refers to the texture of cooked pasta. When cooked "al dente," the pasta is tender but still firm in the middle. The term literally means "to the tooth."

Bake

To cook in dry heat, usually in an oven.

Beat

To combine ingredients and to Incorporate air by manipulating with a spoon or an electric mixer until fluffy.

Blanch

A means of partially cooking food by immersing it in boiling water. After blanching, the cooked food is immediately placed in cold water to stop the cooking process. Always drain blanched foods thoroughly before adding to a dish.

Calorie

A unit of measurement, a calorie is the amount of energy needed to raise the temperature of 1 gram of water by 1 degree Celsius. The number of calories in a food is measured by chemically analyzing the food.

Chop

Chopping consists of cutting food into small pieces. While chopped food doesn't need to be perfectly uniform, the pieces should be roughly the same size.

Deep-fry

To fry in a large amount of oil or melted shortening, lard, or butter so the food is completely covered. In this dry-heat method of cooking, an average of 10 percent of the weight of the food being fried is absorbed as oil.

Dice

Dicing consists of cutting food into small cubes, usually $\frac{1}{4}$" in size or smaller. Unlike chopping, the food should be cut into even-sized pieces.

Dissolve

To immerse a solid in a liquid and heat or manipulate to form a solution in which none of the solid remains.

Drain

Draining consists of drawing off the liquid from a food. Either a colander (a perforated bowl made of metal or plastic) or paper towels can be used to drain food.

Dredge

To dip a food into another mixture, usually made of flour, bread crumbs, or cheese, to completely coat.

Emulsify

To combine an oil and a liquid, either through manipulation or the addition of another ingredient, so they remain suspended in each other.

Flaky

A word describing food texture, usually a pie crust or crust on meat, which breaks apart into flat layers.

Fry

To cook food in hot oil, a dry-heat environment.

Gluten

A protein in wheat, barley, and rye made by combining glutenin and gliadin with a liquid and physical manipulation.

Golden

The color of food when it is browned or quickly sautéed.

Julienne

To julienne food (also called matchstick cutting) means to cut it into very thin strips about $1\frac{1}{2}$"–2" long, with a width and thickness of about $\frac{1}{8}$". Both meat and vegetables can be julienned.

Knead

To manipulate a dough, usually a bread dough, to help develop the gluten in the flour so the bread has the proper texture.

Marinate

To coat foods in an acidic liquid or dry mixture to help break down protein bonds, tenderize, and flavor the food.

Meat thermometer

A thermometer specially labeled to read the internal temperature of meat.

Mince

Mincing consists of cutting food into very small pieces. In general, minced food is cut into smaller pieces than chopped food.

Mortar and pestle

A mortar is a bowl-shaped tool, sometimes made of stone or marble, and a pestle is the round instrument used to grind ingredients in the mortar.

Pan-fry

To quickly fry in a small amount of oil in a saucepan or skillet.

Processed food

Food that has undergone a change from its original form, including, but not limited to, chemical additives in the food; physical manipulation such as cutting, dicing, baking, etc.; ingredients added for flavor and texture; and heavier processing such as preserving for packaged premade meals.

Rancid

Fats can become rancid over time and through exposure to oxygen. The fats oxidize, or break down, and free radicals form, which then exacerbate the process. Rancid fats smell and taste unpleasant.

Reduction

Quickly boiling or simmering liquid to evaporate the water and concentrate the flavor.

Roast

To cook food at relatively high heat in an oven. This is a dry-heat method of cooking, usually used for vegetables and meats.

Roux

A mixture of flour and oil or fat, cooked until the starches in the flour can absorb liquid. It is used to thicken sauces, from white sauce to gumbo.

Sauté

To quickly cook food in a small amount of fat over relatively high heat.

Sear

Searing meat consists of quickly browning it over high heat before finishing cooking it by another method. Searing meat browns the surface and seals in the juices.

Season

To change the flavor of food by adding ingredients like salt, pepper, herbs, and spices.

Shred

Shredding food consists of cutting it into thin strips that are usually thicker than a julienne cut. Meat, poultry, cabbage, lettuce, and cheese can all be shredded.

Simmer

Simmering food consists of cooking it in liquid at a temperature just below the boiling point.

Smoke point

The temperature at which fats begin to break down under heat. The higher the smoke point, the more stable the fat will be while frying and cooking. Butter's smoke point is 300°F and olive oil's is 375°F. Refined oils such as sunflower, peanut, and canola have a higher smoke point, around 440°F.

Vitamins

Vitamins are organic molecules that play a variety of roles in the body including metabolism, chemical reactions, growth, and cellular function. Most vitamins must be ingested, as your body cannot make them.

INDEX

Note: Page numbers in **bold** indicate lists of recipes by category.

A

Apples, recipes featuring, 18, 200, 213

Appliances, 12, 114

Artichokes, 52, 145

Asparagus soup, cashew cream of, 116

Avocados
    Avocado and Shiitake Pot Stickers, 73
    Avocado Bagel Sandwich, 89
    Garden Salad with Avocado and Sprouts, 111
    Gazpacho with Avocado, 121
    Guacamole, 224–25
    Loaded White Bean Avocado Toast, 35

B

Bananas. See also Breads and such
    Banana Bread, 190
    Banana Honey Pancakes, 46
    Easy Banana Date Cookies, 187
    frosty/smoothies with, 194–95, 197, 198, 201, 203
    Peanutty Bananas, 51

Barley, 117, 130

Beans and other legumes
    Black Bean Brownies, 189
    Breakfast Tacos, 43
    Chickpea Cookie Dough, 181
    Chickpea Soft Tacos, 162
    Classic Hummus, 226
    Easiest Black Bean Burger Recipe in the World, 161
    Easy Falafel Patties, 86
    Hummus with Tahini in a Pita Pocket, 92
    Loaded White Bean Avocado Toast, 35
    Pinto Burrito Bowl, 156
    Red Bean Ice Cream Shake, 196
    Roasted Red Pepper Hummus, 214–15
    Savory Chickpea Oatmeal with Garlic Yogurt Sauce, 38
    soups/chili with, 124–27, 132, 135, 137, 139
    Spicy White Bean Citrus Dip, 66
    White Bean Blondies, 177

Berries
    Raspberry Breakfast Bars, 47
    Raspberry Vinaigrette, 211
    smoothies/smoothie bowl with, 197, 198, 200
    Strawberry, Walnut, and Flaxseed Salad, 106–7

Bowls (recipes), 36, 156, 169, 198

Bowls, pots, and pans, 11

Breads and such. See also Sandwiches and wraps
    about: additions for, 19; flatbreads, 90
    Banana Bread, 190
    Loaded White Bean Avocado Toast, 35
    Pear and Pumpkin Breakfast Bread, 30
    Pumpkin Muffins, 20
    Sweet Potato Apple Latkes, 18
    Tomato and Bread Salad (Panzanella), 103
    Zucchini Bread, 19

Breakfast, **15–51**

Buckwheat, portobello mushrooms with beans and, 93

Burritos and burrito bowl, 41, 87, 156

C

Cabbage, 65, 97

Carrots, recipes featuring, 102, 131, 140, 199

Cauliflower soup with coriander, 128

Cheese. See also Pizzas and pizza sauce
    about: eggs with (See Eggs); vegan options/brands, 151
    Chili Cheese Dip, 74
    Garden Quesadillas, 164–65
    Herb-Stuffed Tomatoes with Feta, 26

"Macaroni and Cheese" with Spinach and Tomatoes, 153

Manchego and Potato Tacos with Pickled Jalapeños, 147

salads with, 96, 104, 108

sandwiches with, 82, 84, 85, 89, 94

Spinach and Feta Pie, 159

Chili, vegan, 132–33

Chips, vegetable, 55, 57

Chocolate

Black Bean Brownies, 189

Chickpea Cookie Dough, 181

Chocolate Chip Cookies, 178–79

Chocolate Mocha Ice Cream, 180

Chocolate Nut Bars, 60

Chocolate Tofu Pudding, 186

Cocoa-Nut-Coconut No-Bake Cookies, 193

Foolproof Vegan Fudge, 182

No-Bake Cocoa Balls, 176

pancake wrap and muffins featuring, 21, 23

Peanut Butter Cups, 185

Pumpkin Seed Bark, 183

Sticky Dark Chocolate Pistachio Bars, 188

Triple Chocolate Cupcakes, 191

Vegan Chocolate Hazelnut Spread, 221

White Bean Blondies, 177

"Chorizo" Rice Bowl, 169

Citrus, dip and salsa, 66, 217

Citrus, salads with, 98, 102

Coconut cookies, cocoa-nut no-bake, 193

Coffee, in Chocolate Mocha Ice Cream, 180

Cooking, ingredients, tools/utensils, and terms, 11–13, 114, 231–35. See also Staple recipes

Corn, 61, 146, 167

Cream (heavy), alternative to, 166

Cucumbers

Asian Cucumber Salad, 105

Cucumber Cilantro Salad, 99

Gazpacho with Avocado, 121

Vegan Tzatziki, 72

D

Dates

about: benefits over cane sugar, 203

Carrot and Date Salad, 102

Easy Banana Date Cookies, 187

other desserts/smoothie with, 176, 188, 203

Desserts, **175–93**

Dining hall, 10

Dips, 52, 53, 66, 72, 224–25, 226, 228. See also Hummus; Sauces and dressings

Drinks, shakes, and smoothies, **175**, 194–203

E

Edamame, 139, 144, 173

Eggplant, 109, 158

Egg replacements, 18

Eggs

Cheese and Mushroom Frittata, 24–25

Savory Scrambled Eggs, 29

Spinach and Ricotta Mini Quiches, 27

Sweet Potato Hash Browns with Scrambled Eggs, 34

Very Veggie Omelet, 32–33

F

Falafel patties, 86

Fats/oils, healthy, 7

Fruit, importance of, 7. See also specific fruit

G

Graham Crackers, 63

Granola and granola bars, 28, 56, 69

Grape leaves, stuffed (dolmas), 70

Green beans, 93, 104, 163

Greens, collard/mustard, 130

H

Hummus, 92, 214–15, 226

I

Ingredients, basic, and storing, 13. See also Staple recipes

K

Kale, 39, 55, 210

Kebabs, vegetable, 54

M

Main dishes, **143**–73

Mango Citrus Salsa, 217

Mango ginger ice, vegan, 192

Matcha Smoothie, 201

Mushrooms

    Avocado and Shiitake Pot Stickers, 73

    Cheese and Mushroom Frittata, 24–25

    Grilled Vegetable Antipasto, 109

    Portobello and Pepper Fajitas, 152

    Portobello Pita with Buckwheat and Beans, 93

    Vegetable Kebabs, 54

N

Nachos, 58–59

Nuts and seeds

    about: hemp seed precaution, 35; tahini, 92

    Cashew Cream of Asparagus Soup, 116

    Chewy Granola Bars, 69

    Chocolate Nut Bars, 60

    Cocoa-Nut-Coconut No-Bake Cookies, 193

    DIY Protein Powder, 219

    Foolproof Vegan Fudge, 182

    Homemade Nut Milk, 222

    Homemade Trail Mix, 56

    No-Bake Cocoa Balls, 176

    Peanut Butter Cup Oatmeal, 45

    Peanut Butter Cups, 185

    Peanutty Bananas, 51

    Pumpkin Pie Chia Seed Pudding, 44

    Pumpkin Seed Bark, 183

    Roasted Cashew and Spicy Basil Pesto, 67

    Roasted Pistachios, 62

    smoothies with, 198, 201, 202

    Southwest Almond Soup, 118

    Sticky Dark Chocolate Pistachio Bars, 188

    Strawberry, Walnut, and Flaxseed Salad, 106–7

    Toasted Nut "Cereal," 31

    Trail Mix Crunch, 77

    Vanilla Flax Granola, 28

    Vegan Chocolate Hazelnut Spread, 221

O

Oats and cereal. See also Granola and granola bars; Trail mix

    Cocoa-Nut-Coconut No-Bake Cookies, 193

    High-Fiber Fruity Oatmeal, 17

    Peanut Butter Cup Oatmeal, 45

    Raspberry Breakfast Bars, 47

    Savory Breakfast Quinoa Bowl, 36

    Savory Chickpea Oatmeal with Garlic Yogurt Sauce, 38

    Toasted Nut "Cereal," 31

Olive tapenade, 228

Onions, Simple Scallion Pancakes, 75

Onions, soups featuring, 120, 139

P

Pad Thai dishes, 154–55, 173

Pancakes, etc., 18, 20, 42, 46, 75

Parsnip chips, roasted, 57

Pasta

    Baked Ziti, 151

    Basic Marinara, 209

    Colorful Vegetable and Pasta Salad, 101

    Easy Eggplant Parmigiana, 158

    Easy Pad Thai Noodles, 154–55

    "Macaroni and Cheese" with Spinach and Tomatoes, 153

    Orecchiette with Roasted Peppers, Green Beans, and Pesto, 163

    soups with, 124, 125, 134

    Spaghetti with Sweet Corn, Tomatoes, and Goat Cheese, 168

    Spicy Edamame and Tofu Ramen, 144

Peaches, spiced, brown rice and, 16

Pear and Pumpkin Breakfast Bread, 30

Peppers

    Orecchiette with Roasted Peppers, Green Beans, and Pesto, 163

    Portobello and Pepper Fajitas, 152

    Roasted Red Pepper Hummus, 214–15

    Spicy Jalapeño Poppers, 50

Vegetable Kebabs, 54

Veggie-Stuffed Peppers, 146

Pineapple, frosty with, 194–95

Pizzas and pizza sauce, 149, 157, 172, 223

Plant-based diet

about: dining hall and, 10; grocery shopping, 9; planning meals and meal schedule, 9; this book and, 4, 7

basic ingredients and cooking tips, 13

benefits of, in college, 8

choosing food thoughtfully, 8

defined, 6–7

food categories to include, 7–8

glossary of cooking terms, 231–35

processed/packaged foods and, 6, 9

staples (See Staple recipes)

tips/tricks to start, 9–10

vegan diet and, 7

Popcorn, Italian pesto, 61

Potatoes

"Chorizo" Rice Bowl, 169

Manchego and Potato Tacos with Pickled Jalapeños, 147

Mexican Loaded French Fries, 76

Veggie-Packed Potato Skins, 64

Pots and pans, 11

Pot stickers, 73

Processed foods, 6

Protein, 7

Protein powder, DIY, 219

Pumpkin

about: using fresh instead of canned, 20

bread/muffins, 20, 30

Pumpkin Ale Soup, 123

Pumpkin Pie Chia Seed Pudding, 44

Pumpkin Seed Bark, 183

Q

Quinoa bowl, 36

R

Rice

Brown Rice and Spiced Peaches, 16

"Chorizo" Rice Bowl, 169

Spanish Artichoke and Zucchini Paella, 145

Sun-Dried Tomato Risotto with Spinach and Pine Nuts, 150

Veggies and Rice Soup, 115

S

Salads, **79**, 96–111

Sandwiches and wraps, **79**, 80–95, 147, 161, 162

Sauces and dressings

Basic Balsamic Vinaigrette, 218

Basic Marinara, 209

Easy Homemade Pizza Sauce, 223

Fresh and Spicy Salsa, 207

Garlic Yogurt Sauce, 38

Italian Dressing, 227

Kale Pesto, 210

Mango Citrus Salsa, 217

Raspberry Vinaigrette, 211

Red Garlic Mayonnaise (Rouille), 212

Roasted Cashew and Spicy Basil Pesto, 67

Seitan Buffalo Wings, 171

Smoothies. See Drinks, shakes, and smoothies

Snacks, 10, **49**–77

Soups, **113**–41

Spinach

"Macaroni and Cheese" with Spinach and Tomatoes, 153

other breakfast dishes with, 36, 37, 43

smoothies with, 198, 201

Spinach and Feta Pie, 159

Spinach and Ricotta Mini Quiches, 27

Sun-Dried Tomato Risotto with Spinach and Pine Nuts, 150

Tomato, Mozzarella, and Spinach Salad, 96

Vegan Spinach and Artichoke Dip, 52

Spring rolls, 53, 65

Squash soup, 131

Staple recipes, **205**–28

Stock, vegetable, 216

Stroganoff, vegan, 166

Sweet potatoes

Kale, Sweet Potato, and Tempeh Breakfast Hash, 39

soups with/featuring, 115, 126–27, 129, 137, 140

Sweet Potato and Rosemary Pizza, 157

Sweet Potato Apple Latkes, 18

Sweet Potato Hash Browns with Scrambled Eggs, 34

Sweet Potato Smoothie, 202

T

Tacos, 43, 147, 162

Tempeh

Asian Lettuce Wrap Sandwich, 80–81

Baked Tortilla Wraps, 90

Barbecue Tempeh Pizza, 172

Kale, Sweet Potato, and Tempeh Breakfast Hash, 39

TLT: Tempeh Lettuce Tomato Sandwich, 91

Tofu

about: buying organic, 37

Breakfast Tacos, 43

Chocolate Mocha Ice Cream, 180

Chocolate Tofu Pudding, 186

"Chorizo" Rice Bowl, 169

Easy Pad Thai Noodles, 154–55

Savory Breakfast Quinoa Bowl, 36

snacks with, 65, 73

Spicy Edamame and Tofu Ramen, 144

Strawberry Protein Smoothie, 197

Tofu Breakfast Burrito, 41

Vegan Stroganoff, 166

Vegetable Tofu Scramble, 37

Tomatoes. See also Pasta; Sauces and dressings

Green Bloody Mary, 200

Heirloom Tomato Sandwich, 85

Herb-Stuffed Tomatoes with Feta, 26

salads featuring, 96, 103

soups featuring, 114, 141

soups (other) with, 117, 121, 124–27, 132, 135, 136

Sun-Dried Tomato Risotto with Spinach and Pine Nuts, 150

Tortilla chips, baked, 206

Trail mix, 56, 77

U

Utensils and tools, 11–12, 114

V

Vegan diet, this book and, 7

Vegetables. See also specific vegetables

about: broths, 117; homemade stocks, 216; importance of, 7

Basic Vegetable Stock, 216

salads, **79**, 96–111

soups, **113**–41

Vegetable Kebabs, 54

Vegetable Tofu Scramble, 37

W

Whole grains, importance of, 7

Y

Yogurt, 38, 166, 194–95

Z

Zucchini

Fried Zucchini Sticks, 71

Spanish Artichoke and Zucchini Paella, 145

Veggie-Stuffed Zucchini, 167

Zucchini Bread, 19

Zucchini Soup, 138